TEACHER'S PET PUBLICATIONS

LITPLAN TEACHER PACK
for
The Odyssey
based on the epic work by
Homer

Written by
Barbara M. Linde & Mary B. Collins

© 1996 Teacher's Pet Publications
All Rights Reserved

This **LitPlan** for Homer's
The Odyssey
has been brought to you by Teacher's Pet Publications, Inc.

Copyright Teacher's Pet Publications 1996

Only the student materials in this unit plan
such as worksheets, study questions, assignment sheets and tests
may be reproduced multiple times
for use in the purchaser's classroom.

For any additional copyright questions,
contact Teacher's Pet Publications.

www.tpet.com

TABLE OF CONTENTS - *The Odyssey*

Introduction	10
Unit Objectives	13
Reading Assignment Sheet	14
Unit Outline	15
Study Questions (Short Answer)	19
Quiz/Study Questions (Multiple Choice)	38
Pre-reading Vocabulary Worksheets	71
Lesson One (Introductory Lesson)	95
Nonfiction Assignment Sheet	97
Oral Reading Evaluation Form	99
Writing Assignment 1	106
Writing Assignment 2	113
Writing Assignment 3	117
Writing Evaluation Form	118
Vocabulary Review Activities	107
Extra Writing Assignments/Discussion ?s	111
Unit Review Activities	119
Unit Tests	123
Unit Resource Materials	155
Vocabulary Resource Materials	171

A FEW NOTES ABOUT HOMER AND HIS WORKS

HOMERIC LEGEND. Apart from the historical writings of ancient Israel, the two major pieces of epic literature in Western civilization are the 'Iliad' and the 'Odyssey', two books ascribed to the ancient Greek poet Homer. For audiences today these two works represent a brilliant retelling of myths and legends. For the Greeks of the 7th century BC, however, these books were their history. Their past had been obliterated by the destruction of Mycenaean Civilization. The tales that came down to the Greeks from Homer and other storytellers were regarded by them as authentic narratives of a past they could not otherwise recover.

The individual who has traditionally been credited with putting the ancient Greek legends into writing is Homer. About him nothing certain is known. The later historian Herodotus (5th century BC) said that Homer was a Greek from Ionia on the west coast of Asia Minor. He was perhaps a native of the island of Chios and supposedly lived around 850 BC. Other historians place him closer to 750 BC.

Tradition depicts Homer as a blind minstrel wandering from place to place reciting poems that had come down to him from a very old oral tradition. Many scholars believe that the books as they exist today were not written by a single person and were not put in writing until centuries after they took their present form.

It is probable that much of the epic tradition of the two books was formed in the 200 or 300 years before an alphabet reached Greece in the 9th or 8th century BC. If so, it is possible that Homer used earlier writings to help him, or he could have dictated his poems to someone else because of his blindness or because he was illiterate.

BACKGROUND TO THE 'ILIAD'

The 'Iliad' is a summary in verse of what was apparently a very long war conducted against Troy by the Greeks. As in much myth, there is a kernel of reality behind it. That there was such a war is quite likely. It would have made sense for predecessors of the ancient Greeks to conduct a war against the city in order to gain control of the Dardanelles, the water passage between the Mediterranean and Black seas. Had Troy, located near this waterway, been a hostile power, the destruction of it might have enabled the Greeks to colonize the west coast of Asia Minor. The war probably took place sometime between 1250 and 1185 BC.

For many centuries it was believed that the 'Iliad' was a piece of imaginative and inventive fiction. In 1870, however, the German scholar Heinrich Schliemann began excavations at the place where Troy was believed to have stood. He satisfied himself, and eventually the rest of the world, that there had actually been a war fought there. The excavations revealed that several cities had stood on the spot before the one Homer celebrated.

Altogether, Schliemann and his successors found the ruins of nine cities built atop one another over a period of 3,500 years. Homer's Troy was the seventh city. Ruins of its great walls, 16 feet (5 meters) thick, and flanking towers still remained.

STORY OF THE 'ILIAD'

The 'Iliad' is an amazing tale of heroes and heroines, gods and goddesses. But most of all it is the story of Achilles, his anger and determination, and of his slaying of the Trojan hero Hector.

The purpose of the war was to recover the most beautiful woman in the world, Helen. She was the wife of Menelaus, king of Sparta. But she had been carried off to Troy by Paris, son of King Priam of Troy. Menelaus, naturally, swore vengeance. He called upon the kings and princes of Greece to help him. Among those who responded were Achilles, Ajax, Diomedes, Odysseus, and Nestor. Agamemnon, king of Mycenae and brother of Menelaus, was chosen commander in chief.

After two years of preparation, the Greek fleet of more than 1,000 ships and an army of 100,000 men assembled at the port of Aulis in northeastern Greece. Hence the saying that Helen had the face that launched 1,000 ships.

The fleet was detained at Aulis by a calm sea. Seeking the reason for the delay, they were told by a soothsayer that Agamemnon had killed a stag sacred to the goddess Artemis (or Diana). The wrath of the goddess could only be appeased by the sacrifice of the offender's daughter. Agamemnon was forced to consent. His daughter Iphigenia was led to an altar. The goddess relented at the last minute and snatched Iphigenia away, leaving a deer in her place. Iphigenia became a priestess in the temple of Artemis at Tauris.

With the anger of Artemis appeased, the wind proved favorable and the fleet set sail. They arrived to find the Trojans well prepared. King Priam was too old to fight. He had assembled supplies for a long siege, however, and formed alliances with neighboring princes and chieftains. The city was also protected by impenetrable walls. Its defenders included Hector, Aeneas (of whom the Roman poet Virgil wrote much later), Sarpedon, and other warriors.

For more than nine years the Greeks besieged Troy unsuccessfully. Then Achilles quarreled with Agamemnon and refused to take further part in the conflict. It was the slaying of his friend Patroclus about two thirds of the way through the book that brought Achilles back to the action. He killed Hector in battle, but later he was himself killed-driving the Greeks to despair of ever winning.

It was then that the crafty Odysseus stepped forward with a stratagem. Aided by the goddess Athena, he planned the construction of a huge wooden horse with enough room to contain 100 warriors. Secretly the best warriors were hidden inside. Then the rest of the Greeks boarded ship as though to sail home in defeat. The Trojans thought the horse was a peace offering to Athena. One of the Trojan priests, Laocoön, warned against "Greeks, even bearing gifts." Cassandra, daughter of King Priam, also predicted disaster. She had been given the gift of prophecy but had then been cursed-her prophecies, though always true, would never be believed. Their warnings were shouted down, and a breach in the wall was made to allow the horse to be dragged in.

As the Trojans slept that night, the Greek warriors emerged and signaled the waiting ships to bring back the rest of the Greeks to Troy. Soon thousands of Greeks were swarming into the city. By morning only a mass of ruins remained. Nearly all the inhabitants were slain. Helen returned to her husband, and the Greeks sailed for home. The one whose voyage home took the longest was Odysseus. The adventures of his return trip were told in the second Homeric epic.

THE 'ODYSSEY'

Odysseus, who was later called Ulysses by the Romans, was king of Ithaca, a small island on the west coast of Greece. When summoned to join his fellow chieftains in the war against Troy, he could not bear to leave his young wife, Penelope, and their son, Telemakhos. He therefore pretended to be insane. To convince everyone of his madness, he plowed the sand along the seashore as though it were a field. But Prince Palamedes, who came for him, recognized this as a trick. To prove it, Palamedes placed little Telemakhos in the path of the plow. When Odysseus quickly turned the plow aside to avoid striking his son, all saw that his madness was a pretense. Odysseus could no longer refuse to go to war. Odysseus fitted 12 ships and went to Troy.

By the war's end he had been away from home for ten years. He filled his ships with treasure taken from the Trojans and set sail. Ordinarily the trip from Troy to Ithaca would have taken only a short time. The Greek gods, however, decided that it should take Odysseus ten years to reach his wife and son. During those years he and his men endured a series of hazardous and reable adventures.

Soon after leaving Troy the ships ran into a raging storm. For nine days the winds drove the ships past Ithaca and far off course. On the tenth day they reached the island of the Lotus-Eaters. When a party of men went ashore, they ate of the lotus plants. This magic food made them forget all longing for home. Odysseus had them dragged back to the ships, and again they set sail.

They arrived at the island of the Cyclopes, a race of fierce one-eyed giants. The ever-curious Odysseus set out with 12 men to explore the island. They entered the cave of Polyphemos, the most ferocious of the Cyclopes. He kept them prisoners and devoured six of the men. While the giant slept, Odysseus stole his staff and sharpened it. With this weapon, heated red-hot, he burned out the giant's eye. Odysseus and his men escaped the giant's fury by tying themselves underneath some sheep.

Their next stop was at the Aeolian Isle, a peaceful land where Aeolus, Keeper of the Winds, lived. When they left after a month of relaxation, Aeolus gave them a favorable wind to speed them on their way. The other winds he bound into a leather bag and put on board Odysseus's ship.

The ships sailed smoothly for nine days until Ithaca was in sight. While Odysseus was sleeping his men determined to open the leather bag because they believed it was filled with gold. Upon doing so, the winds were released. They drove the ships back to the Aeolian Isle. This time, however, they were not welcomed. Aeolus believed that men so unlucky must be hated by the gods.

A week later the ships beached at the island of the Laestrygonians, a country of cannibals. Huge men hurled rocks and destroyed 11 of the ships. The crews of all 11 ships perished. Only Odysseus and his ship's crew survived to continue their journey.

Their next stopping place was the island home of Circe, the enchantress. She cast a spell on Odysseus's men, changing them into swine. Odysseus himself was protected by an herb given to him by Hermes, messenger of the gods. When Circe realized he was protected by Hermes, she changed the swine back into men and prevailed upon them all to remain for a year at her palace.

When they decided to leave, she said they must first journey to Hades, the dwelling place of the dead. When they reached Hades, Odysseus met many of his departed comrades, including Achilles. He and his companions were told that many perils still awaited them. There was a chance of reaching home. If they were to do so, however, they must curb their greed when they came to the place where the sun-god Helios pastured his herds. If a single beast were harmed, they would all be doomed.

As they continued their journey, they were forced to sail past the dwelling place of the Sirens, sea nymphs whose singing lured men to certain death. To prevent this from happening, Odysseus had his men put wax in their ears. He had himself tied to the mast so he could listen to the singing.

Once this danger was bypassed, a more ominous one lay ahead. The ship had to sail between Scylla and Charybdis. On one side of a narrow strait Charybdis pulled everything nearby into a vast whirlpool. On the other side Scylla, a six-headed monster, waited to devour anyone who passed by. The ship succeeded in getting through with a burst of speed but not before losing six sailors to the jaws of Scylla.

Those who survived reached the pleasant Isle of the Sun, where Helios pastured his animals. Odysseus wished to sail past it, but the men feared the night seas. They disembarked and were held there for a month by strong winds. As their food supply ran out, the sailors decided they had to kill one of the animals. While Odysseus slept they did so. They were able to sail away without problems, leading them to think they had escaped the wrath of Helios. But Zeus, highest of the gods, replied to the sun-god's request for vengeance by sending a hurricane. It destroyed the ship and crew, leaving Odysseus alone in the sea, clinging to the mast. Ten days later he was carried ashore on the island of Calypso. She kept him prisoner for seven years before he was released through the aid of Athena and Hermes. He made a raft, and after a series of other adventures he finally reached Ithaca.

His problems were not over. He had been gone for 20 years, and no one believed he could still be alive. It was dangerous for him to make himself known because several men were waiting to wed Penelope and gain the kingship. Athena changed Odysseus's appearance and hid in a cave his treasure that he had brought with him from his last stopping place.

Penelope's suitors were staying at the palace, wasting the kingdom's wealth and trying to make the queen choose among them. Telemakhos, the son and heir to the throne, had grown up and spent his time vainly trying to rid the palace of the suitors. Penelope herself put them off by a ruse. She insisted she could not marry anyone until she had finished weaving a shroud for Laertes, the aged father of Odysseus, who was near death. What she wove by day she unraveled each night, so the cloth was never finished. Servants finally gave away her secret to the suitors, however, and they hounded her for an answer.

Odysseus meanwhile found shelter in the hut of his former swineherd. There Telemakhos appeared, having escaped the plan of the suitors to kill him. Odysseus revealed himself to his son, and together they plotted what they would do. Telemakhos returned to the palace, bringing along Odysseus disguised as a beggar. No one recognized Odysseus except his nurse and his aged dog Argos. The animal was too weak to do more than wag its tail before dying.

Penelope did not recognize her husband, but she made him welcome and prepared a room for him. She had by this time decided finally to choose one of the suitors. She decided to make the choice on the basis of a contest among them. The next evening she brought out the great bow Odysseus had left at home, along with its quiver full of arrows. She announced she would marry the man who could drive an arrow through holes in the blades of 12 axes set in a row.

One suitor after another tried, but none could even bend the bow. Odysseus, still clothed as a beggar, stepped forward and asked to test his strength. The suitors thought the idea ridiculous, but Telemakhos gave him the bow. Snatching an arrow, he sent it flying straight through the 12 axe blades. After Odysseus had shown who he was, he and Telemakhos killed all the suitors. The kingdom of Ithaca was restored to him.

ANALYSIS OF THE 'ODYSSEY'

Although set within the circumstances of the Trojan War, the 'Odyssey' is a far different book. With the 'Iliad', from the book itself as well as the archaeological excavations that support it, it is reasonable to infer a real historical event as background. With the 'Odyssey' such an assumption is impossible.

The book is a tale of adventure at sea and of homecoming after a long absence. These two themes have pervaded Western literature ever since the Homeric epic was written, and the story may well have proved a popular one well before Greek history began. The story could just as well have stood on its own without any relation to the conflict of the Greeks with Troy.

The vividly fictional characteristics of the story have not prevented critics, past and present, from seeking to place it in a specific geographic context. Hesiod, who wrote later than Homer, believed that Odysseus and his ships sailed around in the general area of Italy and Sicily, to the west of Ithaca. Later analysts tried to set the wanderings within the Mediterranean Sea generally, while others suggested the Atlantic Ocean as more likely.

The ancient astronomer Eratosthenes (2nd century BC) regarded all such speculations as foolish. For him the world of Odysseus was a completely imaginary one. Indications of this are found within the text itself. Some of the hero's wanderings could well have been based on the even older story of Jason and his Argonauts, who sailed east in search of the golden fleece. It is quite likely that several ancient legends were woven into one continuous epic.

---- Courtesy of Compton's Learning Company

INTRODUCTION

This unit has been designed to develop students' reading, writing, thinking, and language skills through exercises and activities related to *The Odyssey* by Homer. It includes twenty-five lessons, supported by extra resource materials.

The **introductory lesson** introduces students to the idea of dialects through a game-type activity. Following the introductory activity, students are given a transition to explain how the activity relates to the book they are about to read. Following the transition, students are given the materials they will be using during the unit. At the end of the lesson, students begin the pre-reading work for the first reading assignment.

The **reading assignments** are approximately thirty pages each; some are a little shorter while others are a little longer. Students have approximately 15 minutes of pre-reading work to do prior to each reading assignment. This pre-reading work involves reviewing the study questions for the assignment and doing some vocabulary work for 8 to 10 vocabulary words they will encounter in their reading.

The **study guide questions** are fact-based questions; students can find the answers to these questions right in the text. These questions come in two formats: short answer or multiple choice. The best use of these materials is probably to use the short answer version of the questions as study guides for students (since answers will be more complete), and to use the multiple choice version for occasional quizzes. If your school has the appropriate equipment, it might be a good idea to make transparencies of your answer keys for the overhead projector.

The **vocabulary work** is intended to enrich students' vocabularies as well as to aid in the students' understanding of the book. Prior to each reading assignment, students will complete a two-part worksheet for approximately 8 to 10 vocabulary words in the upcoming reading assignment. Part I focuses on students' use of general knowledge and contextual clues by giving the sentence in which the word appears in the text. Students are then to write down what they think the words mean based on the words' usage. Part II nails down the definitions of the words by giving students dictionary definitions of the words and having students match the words to the correct definitions based on the words' contextual usage. Students should then have a thorough understanding of the words when they meet them in the text.

After each reading assignment, students will go back and formulate answers for the study guide questions. Discussion of these questions serves as a **review** of the most important events and ideas presented in the reading assignments.

After students complete reading the work, there is a **vocabulary review** lesson which pulls together all of the fragmented vocabulary lists for the reading assignments and gives students a review of all of the words they have studied.

Following the vocabulary review, a lesson is devoted to the **extra discussion questions/writing assignments**. These questions focus on interpretation, critical analysis and personal response, employing a variety of thinking skills and adding to the students' understanding of the novel.

There is a **group theme project** in this unit. Students are divided into groups, one group for each major theme in the novel. Each group then has a series of assignments to do, all of which lead up to a class-period-long multi-media presentation about that theme. The actual presentation will have three parts: the theme in the novel, the theme in real life today, and a conclusion in which the first two parts are linked together if possible.

There are three **writing assignments** in this unit, each with the purpose of informing, persuading, or having students express personal opinions. The first assignment is to inform: students write compositions about their themes in the novel, based on the research they have done so far. The second assignment is to express personal opinions: students review the personality traits of the characters, pick which character they think they personally are most like, and write a composition explaining how they are like that character. The third assignment is to persuade: students evaluate the group theme projects and decide which they think was the best presentation. They then write a composition persuading the teacher that that presentation was, in fact, the best one.

The **nonfiction reading assignment** is tied in with the Group Theme Project. Students must read nonfiction articles, books, etc. to gather information about their themes in our world today. The information gathered while doing this reading is then incorporated into the students' theme presentations.

The **review lesson** pulls together all of the aspects of the unit. The teacher is given four or five choices of activities or games to use which all serve the same basic function of reviewing all of the information presented in the unit.

The **unit test** comes in two formats: multiple choice or short answer. As a convenience, two different tests for each format have been included. There is also an advanced short answer unit test for advanced students.

There are additional **support materials** included with this unit. The **extra activities section** includes suggestions for an in-class library, crossword and word search puzzles related to the novel, and extra vocabulary worksheets. There is a list of **bulletin board ideas** which gives the teacher suggestions for bulletin boards to go along with this unit. In addition, there is a list of **extra class activities** the teacher could choose from to enhance the unit or as a substitution for an exercise the teacher might feel is inappropriate for his/her class. **Answer keys** are located directly after the **reproducible student materials** throughout the unit. The student materials may be reproduced for use in the teacher's classroom without infringement of copyrights. No other portion of this unit may be reproduced without the written consent of Teacher's Pet Publications, Inc.

The **level** of this unit can be varied depending upon the criteria on which the individual assignments are graded, the teacher's expectations of his/her students in class discussions, and the formats chosen for the study guides, quizzes and test. If teachers have other ideas/activities they wish to use, they can usually easily be inserted prior to the review lesson.

UNIT OBJECTIVES - The *Odyssey*

1. Through reading Homer's *Odyssey*, students will learn about the epic form of literature.

2. Students will demonstrate their understanding of the text on four levels: factual, interpretive, critical and personal.

3. Students will learn about Greek mythology and Greek gods and goddesses.

4. Students will be given the opportunity to practice reading aloud and silently to improve their skills in each area.

7. Students will answer questions to demonstrate their knowledge and understanding of the main events and characters in *The Odyssey* as they relate to the author's theme development.

8. Students will enrich their vocabularies and improve their understanding of the novel through the vocabulary lessons prepared for use in conjunction with the novel.

9. The writing assignments in this unit are geared to several purposes:
    a. To have students demonstrate their abilities to inform, to persuade, or to express their own personal ideas
       Note: Students will demonstrate ability to write effectively to <u>inform</u> by developing and organizing facts to convey information. Students will demonstrate the ability to write effectively to <u>persuade</u> by selecting and organizing relevant information, establishing an argumentative purpose, and by designing an appropriate strategy for an identified audience. Students will demonstrate the ability to write effectively to <u>express personal ideas</u> by selecting a form and its appropriate elements.
    b. To check the students' reading comprehension
    c. To make students think about the ideas presented by the novel
    d. To encourage logical thinking
    e. To provide an opportunity to practice good grammar and improve students' use of the English language.

10. Students will read aloud, report, and participate in large and small group discussions to improve their public speaking and personal interaction skills.

READING ASSIGNMENT SHEET - *The Odyssey*

Date Assigned	Books Assigned	Completion Date
	I-II	
	III-IV	
	V-VI	
	VII-VIII	
	IX	
	X-XII	
	XIII-XIV	
	XV-XVI	
	XVII	
	XVIII-XX	
	XXI-XXII	
	XXIII-XXIV	

UNIT OUTLINE - *The Odyssey*

1 Introduction	2 PVR I-II	3 Study ?s I-II PVR III-IV & V-VI	4 Study ?s III-VI PVR VII-VIII & IX	5 Study ? VII-VIII Library for Nonfiction Reading
6 Study ?s IX PVR X-XII & XIII-XIV	7 Project Assignment	8 Study ?s X-XIV Project Work PVR XV-XVI	9 Study ?s XV-XVI PVR XVII & XVIII-XX	10 Writing Assignment #1
11 Study?s XVII-XX PVR XXI-XXII & XXIII-XXIV	12 Vocabulary	13 Study ?s XXI-XXIV Assign Extra ?s	14 Writing Assignment 2	15 Discussion
16 Nonfiction Reports	17 Group Activity	18 Reports & Discussion	19 Writing Assignment #3	20 Review
21 Test				

Key: P = Preview Study Questions V = Vocabulary Work R = Read

STUDY GUIDE QUESTIONS

SHORT ANSWER STUDY GUIDE QUESTIONS - *The Odyssey*

Book I
1. What is the purpose of the first ten lines of the poem?
2. Why had Odysseus not yet return home from the Trojan war?
3. What does Athena do during a meeting on Mount Olympus?
4. At Odysseus' house in Ithaka, we are introduced to the suitors. What are they doing in the house?
5. What words are used to describe the suitors?
6. How does Athena present herself to Telemakhos?
7. Athena tells Telemakhos to seek information about his father Odysseus from which men?
8. Athena gives Telemakhos one piece of information about his father. What is it?
9. To whom does Athena refer when she says: They all would find death was quick, and marriage a painful matter?
10. What does Athena counsel Telemakhos to do to the suitors?
11. How has Telemakhos changed since the beginning of Book 1, and how does Penelope react?

Book II
12. Why does Telemakhos call the men to assembly?
13. How has Penelope managed to hold off the suitors' demands for the past four years?
14. What sign does Zeus send to the assembly, and what is its meaning?
15. What does Telemakhos plan to do now?

Book III
NOTICE when Nestor is telling Telemakhos what he knows of the return of the Akhaians) he describes a quarrel between "the two sons of Artreus." These are Agamemnon and Menelaus. The quarrel had to do with some sacrifice to the gods which was evidently not satisfactory, causing Athena to get mad and causing some of the Akhaians to have troublesome homecomings. Notice Agamemnon is also called Atreides (line 193). Nestor also makes clear to Telemakhos that a son's duty is to preserve the honor of a father's house. He also holds up the example of Orestes as has Athena.

16. Where does the action in Book III take place?
17. Where is Athena during this part of the story?
18. Describe Nestor.
19. What happens at the homecoming of Agamemnon?
20. What does Orestes do?

NOTICE (lines 309-310) Klytaimnestra has been killed, yet her death is not described. Nor is Elektra (sister of Orestes) ever mentioned. Who, according to myth, encouraged Orestes to commit the murders.

Odyssey Short Answer Study Questions Page 2

21. How does Nestor help Telemakhos?
22. Who accompanies Telemakhos to Sparta to the house of Menelaus?

Book IV
23. What is the setting of Book IV?
24. How is Telemakhos' identity revealed to Menelaus?
25. Menelaus describes his stay in Egypt to Telemakhos. During his stay there, who told Menelaus where Odysseus was detained?
26. According to Menelaus' informant, where was Odysseus?
27. Why is Menelaus to go to the Elysian Field instead of dying as other mortals do?
28. The scene shifts to the home of Odysseus. What plan do the suitors devise against Telemakhos?
29. Identify the leading men of the suitors.
30. Who comforts Penelope after she learns of the suitors' plan and the journey of Telemakhos?

Book V
31. What is Zeus' command to Kalypso?
32. Which god or goddess brings Zeus' command to Kalypso?
33. What happens to Odysseus on the eighteenth day, just as he sights the shores of Skheria?
34. What help does Ino give to Odysseus?
35. What happens to Odysseus at the end of Book V?

Book VI
36. Who discovers Odysseus on the shore?
37. Why was this person near the river?
38. What does Odysseus' discoverer do for him?
39. Why doesn't his benefactor bring Odysseus to the palace in person?

Book VII
40. Whom does Odysseus approach for assistance when he enters the palace?
41. What does Alkinoos offer to Odysseus so he could stay with the Phaiakians?

Book VIII
42. Odysseus is insulted by Seareach. What does he accuse Odysseus of being? Why?
43. With Athena's help, what athletic feat does Odysseus accomplish?
44. Odysseus brags that he is an accomplished athlete but allows one test where the Phaiakians would likely win. To which test does he refer? Why?
45. Why do you think Homer interrupts the narrative to have Demodokos sing about the love of Ares and Aphrodite?

Odyssey Short Answer Study Questions Page 3

Book IX
NOTE: In books IX through XII Homer provides us with a flashback to supply background information. He has Odysseus identify himself and tell the Phaikians of his wanderings since he left Troy.

46. Which encounter does Odysseus and his men have before Polyphemos?
47. Why is it necessary for Odysseus to take some of his men by force away from the land of the Lotos-Eaters?
48. What kind of creature does Odysseus encounter in the next land?
49. Why does Odysseus lead his men into Polyphemos' cave?
50. What happens when Polyphemos finds Odysseus and his men in the cave?
51. How is Odysseus able to wound Polyphemos?
52. How do Odysseus and his remaining men escape from the cave?
53. How is the craftiness and cunning of Odysseus revealed in this escape?
54. Why does Odysseus reveal his name to Polyphemos after he has escaped?

Book X
55. What natural phenomenon is controlled by Aeolus?
56. How does Aeolus show his goodwill when Odysseus is about to leave?
57. Odysseus and his men come within sight of Ithaka. Why do they not land?
58. Odysseus asks for further help from Aeolus. What is his reply?
59. Describe the Laestrygonians.
60. Who helps Odysseus outwit Kirke?
61. Why must Odysseus visit the house of Hades?

Book XI
62. How does Odysseus gain access to the underworld?
63. What does Odysseus promise Elpenor?
64. Why does Odysseus not let his mother come near the blood?
65. What does Teiresias tell Odysseus?
66. Who comes to speak to Odysseus after all the souls of the women have departed?
67. What does this person tell Odysseus?
68. Many other heroes speak to Odysseus, and he learns of their fates. What happens to Tantalos?
69. What punishment is Sisyphos enduring?

Book XII
70. How do the Seirines destroy men, and how do Odysseus and his men avoid destruction?
71. What are Skylla and Kharybdis?
72. What happens to Odysseus' companions?
73. What happens to Odysseus?

Odyssey Short Answer Study Questions Page 4

Book XIII
74. How does Poseidon react when he discovers that the Phaiakians have aided Odysseus in reaching Ithaka?
75. How does Odysseus react when he awakens on land?
76. Why does Athena now reveal herself to Odysseus?
77. Where does Athena send Odysseus first?
78. What task does Athena first set out to do?

Book XIV
79. Who is Eumaeus?
80. Why does Odysseus hide his identity from Eumaeus?
81. Does Eumaeus believe Odysseus' tale?

Book XV
82. Telemakhos receives an omen as he is about to depart. What is it, and what does it mean?
83. Who journeys to Ithaka with Telemakhos and his companions?
84. Odysseus has a plan that he shares with Eumaeus. What is it?
85. What is Eumaeus' reaction to Odysseus' idea?
86. How did Eumaeus come to be swineherd for Odysseus?
87. Which are the two signs that the gods send to Telemakhos and Odysseus?

Book XVI
88. What action does Odysseus take?
89. What instructions does Odysseus give to Telemakhos?

Book XVII
90. Penelope greets Telemakhos when he arrives home and asks to hear his news. Telemakhos' version and that of Theoklymenos differ. How are they different?
91. Identify the speaker: "See now how the rascal comes on leading a rascal about: like guides what is like itself, just as a god does."
92. What two physical assaults does Odysseus endure?
93. Who is Argus, and what happens to him?

Book XVIII
94. What occurs between Odysseus and Iros? Why?
95. What reward does Odysseus (still disguised) give to Amphinomos for helping him?
96. What does Penelope do that makes Odysseus happy?
97. How does Odysseus come to be a target for the foot stool again?

Odyssey Short Answer Study Questions Page 5

Book XIX
98. What action does Odysseus take now?
99. How does Eurykleia discover the identity of Odysseus?
100. What contest does Penelope devise to test the suitors?

Book XX
101. Who tells Odysseus (the beggar) that if Odysseus were to return he would help to destroy the suitors?
102. While the suitors are plotting Telemakhos' death they see an omen. What is it, and what does it mean?
103. Who warns that evil will come to the suitors before he leaves the house?

Book XXI
104. Who, other than Odysseus, has the strength and power to string the bow?
105. To what men does Odysseus reveal his identity?
106. What is Odysseus' plan.

Book XXII
107. Which men does Odysseus spare from the slaughter?
108. What happens to the disloyal serving women?

Book XXIII
109. Why is Penelope so hesitant to greet her husband?
110. How does Penelope test Odysseus?

Book XXIV
111. Where does Odysseus go next?
112. Why does Laertes wear rags and not bathe?
113. What does Athena do when the families of the dead suitors attack Odysseus?
114. In the oral epic there is a lot of repetition. List some lines that have been used by the poet repeatedly.

ANSWER KEY SHORT ANSWER STUDY GUIDE QUESTIONS - *Odyssey*

Book I

1. What is the purpose of the first ten lines of the poem?
    The first ten lines of the poem are an invocation to the muse of epic poetry. Homer pretends that the muse is speaking through him, and asks that his memory remain accurate.

2. Why had Odysseus not yet return home from the Trojan war?
    He had angered the god Poseidon by blinding Poseidon's son, Polyphemos. Poseidon has placed obstacles in his way and Odysseus has not yet been able to return home.

3. What does Athena do during a meeting on Mount Olympus?
    During Poseidon's absence, she asks Zeus to let Odysseus return home. She suggests that Hermes be sent to tell Kalypso to release Odysseus. She will go to Ithaka and talk to Odysseus' son, Telemakhos, and tell him where to go to find out information about his father. Zeus agrees.

4. At Odysseus' house in Ithaka, we are introduced to the suitors. What are they doing in the house?
    They are waiting for Penelope to make up her mind which one of them she will marry. While waiting, they are eating and drinking all of the food in the house.

5. What words are used to describe the suitors?
    Words like lusty, arrogant, young bloods, and gluttons are used.

6. How does Athena present herself to Telemakhos?
    She comes to his home disguised as Mentes, an old friend of his father.

7. Athena tells Telemakhos to seek information about his father Odysseus from which men?
    He should seek information from Nestor in Pylos and Menelaus in Sparta.

8. Athena gives Telemakhos one piece of information about his father. What is it?
    She tells him that Odysseus is not dead, but is detained somewhere on the seas. She says Odysseus can and will do anything to get home.

9. To whom does Athena refer when she says: They all would find death was quick, and marriage a painful matter?
    She refers to the suitors.

10. What does Athena counsel Telemakhos to do to the suitors?
    She suggests killing them either openly or by treachery.

11. How has Telemakhos changed since the beginning of Book 1, and how does Penelope react?
    He has become more assertive, referring to himself as the man of the house. She looks at him in wonder.

Book II

12. Why does Telemakhos call the men to assembly?
    He wants to publicly address the problem of the suitors. They are literally eating and drinking him out of house and home. (There is a strict ritual of guest and host in The Odyssey. A guest, especially a stranger, brings news and praise to a house and a host receives a guest with offers of refreshment and gifts. The suitors are disrespectful of the relationship between host and guests, at least in Odysseus' house, and this has angered the gods. The Greek gods were said to sometimes show up as beggars at a house to test the hospitality of a man. Thus the suitors have broken the rule of hospitality in a land and time when hospitality could mean the difference between life and death.

13. How has Penelope managed to hold off the suitors' demands for the past four years?
    She appeals to them to let her finish a death shroud for Laertes, father of Odysseus, so that when he dies she can properly bind him as is her duty (since his wife is dead). She weaves the shroud by day and then unweaves it at night to prolong having to answer to the suitors. They have been told of her deceit, and are angry at her refusal to choose a husband.

14. What sign does Zeus send to the assembly, and what is its meaning?
    Zeus launches a pair of eagles who drop on the heads of the crowd (A death omen). Halitherses, who is skilled in reading birdflight, tells them it means that Odysseus is alive and will return soon. When he does, the suitors will be killed.

15. What does Telemakhos plan to do now?
    Telemakhos plans to take a ship and twenty men and sail to Sparta and Pylos in search of news of his father. He keeps this news secret until time for his departure. Then Athena causes the suitors to fall into a deep sleep, and sends a good wind to start Telemakhos on his journey.

Book III
NOTICE when Nestor is telling Telemakhos what he knows of the return of the Akhaians (Greeks) he describes a quarrel between "the two sons of Artreus." These are Agamemnon and Menelaus. The quarrel had to do with some sacrifice to the gods which was evidently not satisfactory, causing Athena to get mad and causing some of the Akhaians to have troublesome homecomings. Notice Agamemnon is also called Atreides (line 193). Nestor also makes clear to

Telemakhos that a son's duty is to preserve the honor of a father's house. He also holds up the example of Orestes as has Athena.

16. Where does the action in Book III take place?
    The action takes place at Pylos, Telemakhos' first stop on his search for information about his father.

17. Where is Athena during this part of the story?
    She has accompanied Telemakhos on his journey, in the disguise of Mentor. When Telemakhos makes preparations to spend the night in Nestor's palace, she changes to a vulture and flies away. Nestor interprets this as a sign of her favor for Telemakhos, and prepares a sacrificial offering to her.

18. Describe Nestor.
    Nestor is an old friend of Odysseus' who also fought in the Trojan war. He offers food and drink to Telemakhos and his men, even before asking their names. Nestor then tells stories about Agamemnon and Menelaus.

19. What happens at the homecoming of Agamemnon?
    He is murdered by his wife, Klytaimnestra, and her lover, Aigisthos.

20. What does Orestes do?
    He avenges his father's death. "Orestes killed the snake who killed his father. He gave his hateful mother and soft man a tomb together, and proclaimed the funeral day a festival day for all the Argive people."

NOTICE (lines 309-310) Klytaimnestra has been killed, yet her death is not described. Nor is Elektra (sister of Orestes) ever mentioned. Who, according to myth, encouraged Orestes to commit the murders.

21. How does Nestor help Telemakhos?
    Nestor gives Telemakhos a cart and a team of horses to take him on his inland journey.

22. Who accompanies Telemakhos to Sparta to the house of Menelaus?
    Peisistratos, son of Nestor, does.

Book IV
23. What is the setting of Book IV?
    The setting is the home of Menelaus in Sparta.

24. How is Telemakhos' identity revealed to Menelaus?
   Menelaus, unaware of the identity of his visitors, speaks of his grief and losses during and after the Trojan War. When he mentions Odysseus, Telemakhos begins to weep. Helen, the wife of Menelaus, enters the room and recognizes Telemakhos immediately, even though she has never met him. Apparently, Telemakhos's resemblance to Odysseus is quite striking, and he is easily recognizable to those who knew Odysseus.

25. Menelaus describes his stay in Egypt to Telemakhos. During his stay there, who told Menelaus where Odysseus was detained?
   Proteus, the Old Man of the Sea, did.

26. According to Menelaus' informant, where was Odysseus?
   He was being detained on an island by the nymph Kalypso.

27. Why is Menelaus to go to the Elysian Field instead of dying as other mortals do?
   He is the husband of Helen, and son-in-law of Zeus, and he will not die.

28. The scene shifts to the home of Odysseus. What plan do the suitors devise against Telemakhos?
   They put a ship in the harbor in order to ambush and kill him when he returns.

29. Identify the leading men of the suitors.
   They are Antinoos and Eurymachos.

30. Who comforts Penelope after she learns of the suitors' plan and the journey of Telemakhos?
   Athena disguised as Penelope's sister Ipthime, comes to Penelope in a dream and calms her fears about Telemakhos. However, she will not allay Penelope's fears about Odysseus.

Book V
31. What is Zeus' command to Kalypso?
   She is to release Odysseus and allow him to return home. (Zeus adds that Odysseus is to have no help from gods or men, and must make his own raft from trees on Kalypso's island. Kalypso presents the idea to Odysseus as her own. She gives him an axe to use for cutting. When he is ready to leave, she gives him food and clothing.)

32. Which god or goddess brings Zeus' command to Kalypso?
   Hermes does.

33. What happens to Odysseus on the eighteenth day, just as he sights the shores of Skheria?
    Poseidon, returning from a vacation in Ethiopia, sees the raft. In a rage he creates a storm which destroys the raft.

34. What help does Ino give to Odysseus?
    She gives him her magic veil which allows him to survive the long swim to Skheria.

35. What happens to Odysseus at the end of Book V?
    The ocean currents take him to the mouth of a river. He swims up the river and lands safely on the shore. Odysseus tosses Ino's veil back into the sea, makes a bed of leaves, and falls asleep.

Book VI
36. Who discovers Odysseus on the shore?
    Nausikaa, daughter of Alkinoos, ruler of Skheria, found Odysseus.

37. Why was this person near the river?
    Athena had come to her in a dream and chided her for having soiled clothes. According to Athena, no one will want to marry a girl who has piles of dirty laundry around. When she awoke in the morning, Nausikaa gathered the dirty laundry, and she and her maids set out for the river to wash the clothes.

38. What does Odysseus' discoverer do for him?
    She gives him food and olive oil. Then she guides him to the city and tells him how to approach her parents.

39. Why doesn't his benefactor bring Odysseus to the palace in person?
    Nausikaa is of marriageable age, and does not wish to appear to favor a foreign man when there are noble Phaiakians to choose as a husband. She does not want to cause any gossip and resentment among her possible suitors.

Book VII
40. Whom does Odysseus approach for assistance when he enters the palace?
    As instructed by both Na and Athena, Odysseus grasps the knees of Arete, the wife of Alkinoos.

41. What does Alkinoos offer to Odysseus so he could stay with the Phaiakians?
    He offers him marriage with Nausikaa.

Book VIII
42. Odysseus is insulted by Seareach. What does he accuse Odysseus of being? Why?
    Laodamas urges Odysseus to compete in the games, but Odysseus refuses, explaining that he has suffered too much and longs only to be home. Seareach accuses Odysseus of being a man concerned only with business and profits, and not with being an athlete. (Note that athletic stamina was highly important to the Greeks, the founders of the Olympic games. Doing business was necessary, but the typical Greek of the time had a disregard for people who earned their money by buying and selling.

43. With Athena's help, what athletic feat does Odysseus accomplish?
    He throws a heavy discus the farthest distance.

44. Odysseus brags that he is an accomplished athlete but allows one test where the Phaiakians would likely win. To which test does he refer? Why?
    Odysseus says he would not perform well in a foot race, since he has been battered by the sea for so many days.

45. Why do you think Homer interrupts the narrative to have Demodokos sing about the love of Ares and Aphrodite?
    Homer wants to remind his own listeners that storytellers are blessed by the Muse and should be treated well.

Book IX
NOTE: In books IX through XII Homer provides us with a flashback to supply background information. He has Odysseus identify himself and tell the Phaikians of his wanderings since he left Troy.

46. Which encounter does Odysseus and his men have before Polyphemos?
    They sack Ismaros and take the Kikones' wives and possessions.

47. Why is it necessary for Odysseus to take some of his men by force away from the land of the Lotos-Eaters?
    The lotos fruit contained a magical drug that made them want to stay and eat more.

48. What kind of creature does Odysseus encounter in the next land?
    He encounters the Kyklopes, one-eyed giants who are quite lawless.

49. Why does Odysseus lead his men into Polyphemos' cave?
    Odysseus is both curious and hungry. He steals some of the animals and cheese. Being the warrior and explorer that he is, Odysseus is curious to see the owner of the cave; this is his mistake. Also, keep in mind the Greek custom of offering

food to strangers. It is quite possible that Odysseus expected this kind of treatment from the Kyklopes.

50. What happens when Polyphemos finds Odysseus and his men in the cave?
    Polyphemos is quite angry at the intrusion. He scoffs at Odysseus' request for courtesy. Instead, Polyphemos devours two of Odysseus' men.

51. How is Odysseus able to wound Polyphemos?
    Odysseus and his men prepare a log sharpened on one end. When Polyphemos returns to the cave with his flock, Odysseus offers him the potent wine he has brought along. Polyphemos drinks it and falls into a stupor. Then the men heat the point of the log and drive it into his eye while he sleeps.

52. How do Odysseus and his remaining men escape from the cave?
    They lash themselves to the bellies of the rams and escape when Polyphemos lets the sheep out in the morning.

53. How is the craftiness and cunning of Odysseus revealed in this escape?
    He brings along the potent wine, which he uses to drug Polyphemos. He announces that his name is Nobody. Polyphemos calls to the other Kyklopes that Nobody has injured him, so none of them come to his aid.

54. Why does Odysseus reveal his name to Polyphemos after he has escaped?
    He is a hero of the Trojan War and a brave and proud man. He wants Polyphemos to know who has bested him.

Book X
55. What natural phenomenon is controlled by Aeolus?
    He controls the winds.

56. How does Aeolus show his goodwill when Odysseus is about to leave?
    Aeolus gives Odysseus a bull's hide sewn into a bag. It contains the destructive storm winds. As long as the bag remains closed, Odysseus will have smooth sailing.

57. Odysseus and his men come within sight of Ithaka. Why do they not land?
    The men think the bag from Aeolus contains treasure that Odysseus is keeping for himself. While Odysseus is sleeping, they open the bag. The winds escape and they are blown back to the Aeolan island.

58. Odysseus asks for further help from Aeolus. What is his reply?
    Aeolus believes the gods hate Odysseus and that is why he has been blown back to the island. He refuses to help anyone who is in disfavor with the gods.

59. Describe the Laestrygonians.
    They are giants and cannibals.

60. Who helps Odysseus outwit Kirke?
    Hermes helps Odysseus.

61. Why must Odysseus visit the house of Hades?
    He must consult with the blind prophet Teiresias, who will tell Odysseus all he needs to know about getting home.

Book XI
62. How does Odysseus gain access to the underworld?
    Odysseus follows Kirke's instructions and digs a votive pit. He pours libations to the dead and sacrifices the lamb and ewe given him by Kirke.

63. What does Odysseus promise Elpenor?
    He promises to return to Kirke's island and bury Elpenor's body.

64. Why does Odysseus not let his mother come near the blood?
    He is waiting for Teiresias to speak to him first.

65. What does Teiresias tell Odysseus?
    He tells him that his homecoming will be a hard one and gives Odysseus a warning not to harm the sheep and cattle of Helios on the island of Thrinakia. If they are harmed, Teiresias says he will lose all his companions and find trouble at home upon his long-delayed return. He also tells Odysseus that when he has put his home in order he must set out again on a journey and find a land where people do not know of the sea or the use of an oar, and there he must make generous sacrifices to Poseidon. If he does this, he will be assured of a peaceful life and seaborne death.

66. Who comes to speak to Odysseus after all the souls of the women have departed?
    Agamemnon does.

67. What does this person tell Odysseus?
    He describes how his wife Klytaimnestra and her lover Aigsthos murdered him and his companions at their homecoming.

68. Many other heroes speak to Odysseus, and he learns of their fates.
   What happens to Tantalos?
   > He is tortured by having an abundance of food and water always just beyond his grasp, so that he is constantly starved.

69. What punishment is Sisyphos enduring?
   > Sisyphos must constantly push a large boulder up a steep hill. As soon as the boulder reaches the top of the hill, the gods send it rolling down, and he must start his labors all over again.

Book XII

70. How do the Seirines destroy men, and how do Odysseus and his men avoid destruction?
   > Their singing entices men to land on their island, where, enchanted, they die on the beach. Odysseus orders his men to plug their ears with beeswax so they won't hear the singing. He also orders them to lash him to the mast, so that he can hear the Seirines' songs and not succumb to them.

71. What are Skylla and Kharybdis?
   > They are two horrible monsters who destroy men as they sail through the narrow straight between them. Skylla has six heads with which she snatches up men from their ships and eats them. Kharybdis is a whirlpool that sucks down men and ships, destroying them.

72. What happens to Odysseus' companions?
   > The crew members are hungry and ignore Odysseus' order not to harm Helios' sheep. Enraged, Helios threatens to shine only in the underworld unless Zeus punishes the men. The men and ships are able to leave the island, but once they are at sea, Zeus creates a hurricane that destroys the ships and drowns all but Odysseus.

73. What happens to Odysseus?
   > Odysseus manages to lash pieces of the mast and keel together to create a small raft. He drifts north, back to Kharybdis and Skylla. His raft is consumed by Kharybdis, but Odysseus grabs onto a branch of a fig tree and saves himself. He hangs there until the whirlpool spouts, releasing his raft. Then Odysseus rows furiously and, nine days later, arrives at Kalypso's island.

Book XIII

74. How does Poseidon react when he discovers that the Phaiakians have aided Odysseus in reaching Ithaka?
   > Poseidon is angry that Odysseus has reached Ithaka easily and with great presents. He punishes the Phaiakians by turning their ship to stone just as it reaches their

harbor. He then erects a ring of high mountains around the island, cutting them off from their livelihood.

75. How does Odysseus react when he awakens on land?
    Odysseus does not recognize his homeland. He thinks the Phaiakians have left him on an undisclosed shore. It is not until he meets Athena, disguised as a swineherd, that he discovers he is indeed home.

76. Why does Athena now reveal herself to Odysseus?
    She wants to help him plan his revenge on Penelope's suitors.

77. Where does Athena send Odysseus first?
    She sends him disguised as a beggar to his loyal swineherd.

78. What task does Athena first set out to do?
    She goes to Lakedaimon to bring Telemakhos home.

Book XIV
79. Who is Eumaios?
    He is Odysseus' faithful swineherd.

80. Why does Odysseus hide his identity from Eumaios?
    He does not want it known that he has arrived home, and he wants to test Eumaios' loyalty to his master.

81. Does Eumaios believe Odysseus' tale?
    Eumaios believes all but the part about Odysseus still being alive.

Book XV
82. Telemakhos receives an omen as he is about to depart. What is it, and what does it mean?
    A mountain eagle holding a white goose in its talons flies to the right over the horses. Helen interprets the sign to mean that Odysseus will soon return to Ithaka and take revenge on the suitors.

83. Who journeys to Ithaka with Telemakhos and his companions?
    Theoklymenos, a descendant of Melampus, of a noble Greek family, asks to join them. He is a gifted prophet and is also a fugitive from Argos, where he has murdered his cousin.

84. Odysseus has a plan that he shares with Eumaios. What is it?
    Odysseus plans to go to his own house and ask for a job as a servant for the suitors.

85. What is Eumaios' reaction to Odysseus' idea?

> Eumaios tries to discourage Odysseus, saying the suitors prefer young boys. He fears that the suitors may mistreat such an old beggar. Eumaios suggests that Odysseus stay where he is. He assures Odysseus that Telemakhos will offer him care and protection when he returns.

86. How did Eumaios come to be swineherd for Odysseus?

> Eumaios is really of noble lineage. He was kidnapped as a child by his nurse, who ran off with Phoinikian traders. When she fell overboard, (possibly killed by the gods) the Phoinikians sold him to Laertes.

87. Which are the two signs that the gods send to Telemakhos and Odysseus?

> An eagle carrying a white goose flies past Telemakhos on the right side and a falcon carrying a pigeon flies past Odysseus on the right side. These symbolize that both men will catch the prey (suitors) they are after.

Book XVI

88. What action does Odysseus take?

> At first, Odysseus urges Telemakhos to act against the suitors on his father's behalf. Telemakhos replies that, since he has no brothers to help him, this is not feasible. At Athena's suggestion, he reveals his true identity to Telemakhos.

89. What instructions does Odysseus give to Telemakhos?

> He tells him to go home and wait for his father's arrival as a beggar. He warns Telemakhos not to interfere if the suitors are rude, but to wait for the signal to hide all weapons except their own. He also reminds Telemakhos not to let anyone know that he (Odysseus) has returned.

Book XVII

90. Penelope greets Telemakhos when he arrives home and asks to hear his news. Telemakhos' version and that of Theoklymenos differ. How are they different?

> They differ in the news of Odysseus's current whereabouts. Since Telemakhos is under orders from his father not to reveal his presence, he ends his version saying that Odysseus is still a prisoner on the island of Kalypso. Theoklymenos, the prophet, says that Odysseus is present on the island and is about to avenge himself.

91. Identify the speaker: "See now how the rascal comes on leading a rascal about: like guides what is like itself, just as a god does."

> It is spoken by Melanthios, disloyal goatheard of Odysseus, to Emaious and Odysseus.

92. What two physical assaults does Odysseus endure?
> First he is kicked by Melanthious at the fountain and then he is hit with a footstool thrown by Antinoos in his own house.

93. Who is Argus, and what happens to him?
> Argus is Odysseus' beloved hunting dog. He recognizes Odysseus, disguised as a beggar, when Odysseus and Eumaios approach the house. He is old, and now dies, happy that he has seen his master one last time.

Book XVIII
94. What occurs between Odysseus and Iros? Why?
> They have a fist fight to decide which beggar may stay and which may leave. Odysseus wins with one powerful blow, and he drags Iros outside the courtyard where he orders him to scare away stray pigs and dogs.

95. What reward does Odysseus (still disguised) give to Amphinomos for helping him?
> Odysseus, while concealing his true identity, warns Amphinomos of the fate awaiting the suitors.

96. What does Penelope do that makes Odysseus happy?
> She speaks to the suitors, hinting that there may soon be a marriage, but that in times past suitors of a noble woman always offered great gifts as well as cattle and sheep. So the suitors send for glorious presents to be brought to Penelope. Odysseus is happy that his cunning wife has enriched his house. It may be supposed that her description of marriage to any of the suitors as "hateful" would also please Odysseus.

97. How does Odysseus come to be a target for the foot stool again?
> Eurymachos insults Odysseus and accuses him of preferring to beg rather than work. Odysseus boasts that in any contest between them, working or fighting, he would be the better man. Eurymachos hurls the footstool after Odysseus points out that Eurymachos considers himself brave and powerful but has only cowardly and little men around him for comparison.

Book XIX
98. What action does Odysseus take now?
> Odysseus reminds Telemakhos of the plan to remove the weapons from the hall. The two of them carry out this part of the plan. As they work, Athena holds a lamp that shines on the walls.

99. How does Eurykleia discover the identity of Odysseus?
   Eurykleia had been Odysseus' nursemaid when he was a child. Now she recognizes a scar on his leg when she washes his feet. Odysseus orders her to be silent and not reveal his identity, and she complies.

100. What contest does Penelope devise to test the suitors?
   She remembers a contest which Odysseus used to set up, where he would send an arrow through the iron of twelve axes. She decides whoever can string the great bow of Odysseus and repeat this feat shall be her husband.

Book XX
101. Who tells Odysseus (the beggar) that if Odysseus were to return he would help to destroy the suitors?
   Philoitios the cowherd does.

102. While the suitors are plotting Telemakhos' death, they see an omen. What is it, and what does it mean?
   They see an eagle with a dove in its claws crossing their path from the left. Amphinomos says the sign means that their plan will not work.

103. Who warns that evil will come to the suitors before he leaves the house?
   Theoklymenos does.

Book XXI
104. Who, other than Odysseus, has the strength and power to string the bow?
   Telemakhos does. He would have strung the bow on his fourth attempt, but a signal from his father stopped him.

105. To what men does Odysseus reveal his identity?
   He reveals his identity to Eumaios and Philoitios.

106. What is Odysseus' plan?
   Eumaios will give the bow to Odysseus, and then tell the maids to stay in their quarters. Philoitios will close the door to the courtyard and block off the escape route.

Book XXII
107. Which men does Odysseus spare from the slaughter?
   He spares Phemios, the minstrel, and Medon, the herald.

108. What happens to the disloyal serving women?
    Telemakhos takes them outside, after they have cleared and cleaned the house of their dead lovers. He ties them up against the round house and with a rope hangs all of them.

Book XXIII
109. Why is Penelope so hesitant to greet her husband?
    She fears it is a trick or a device of the gods. She wants to be sure it is really Odysseus.

110. How does Penelope test Odysseus?
    She tells the servants to bring out his bed, and then waits for his reaction. (His bed has been built from a rooted tree and cannot be moved). When Odysseus protests about moving the bed, she realizes he is truly her husband.

Book XXIV
111. Where does Odysseus go next?
    He, accompanied by Telemakhos, Eumaios, and Philoitios, goes to the home of Laertes.

112. Why does Laertes wear rags and not bathe?
    He is despondent that he will never see his son again.

113. What does Athena do when the families of the dead suitors attack Odysseus?
    She makes both sides pledge peace, and threatens them with the wrath of Zeus.

114. In the oral epic there is a lot of repetition. List some lines that have been used by the poet repeatedly.
    *"when they had put aside their desire for eating and drinking"
    *"grey-eyed Athena"
    *"Dawn's rosy fingers"
    *"But when the young Dawn showed again with her rosy fingers"
    *"They would all find death was quick and marriage a painful matter"
    *"what sort of wold has escaped your teeth's barrier?"
    *"Son of Laertes and seed of Zeus, resourceful Odysseus"
    *"A maidservant brought water for them and poured it from a splendid and golden pitcher, holding it above a silver basin for them to wash, and she pulled a polished table before them."
    *"A grave housekeeper brought in the bread and served it to them, adding many god things to it, generous with her provisions."
    *"What man are you and whence? Where is your city? Your parents?"

STUDY GUIDE/QUIZ QUESTIONS - *The Odyssey*
Multiple Choice Format

Book I

1. True or False: The first ten lines of the poem are an invocation to the muse of epic poetry. Homer pretends that the muse is speaking through him and asks that his memory remain accurate.
    A. True
    B. False

2. Why had Odysseus not yet returned home from the Trojan War?
    A. His boat had been damaged and he put into a port to have it fixed. The parts he needed were not available, so he had to set his men to making them. The process was taking a long time.
    B. He had angered the god Poseidon by blinding Poseidon's son, Polyphemos. Poseidon has placed obstacles in his way and Odysseus has not yet been able to return home.
    C. He stayed in Troy to help repair the damage done by the war. He felt it was the honorable thing to do.
    D. Odysseus was a man of adventure. He didn't really want to return home to his quiet, dull life, so he set out to have adventures instead.

3. During Poseidon's absence, Athena asks Zeus to let Odysseus return home. She suggests that Hermes be sent to tell Kalypso to release Odysseus. She will go to Ithaka and talk to Odysseus' son, Telemakhos, and tell him where to go to find out information about his father. How does Zeus reply?
    A. He agrees.
    B. He disagrees.

4. At Odysseus' house in Ithaka, we are introduced to the suitors. What are they doing in the house?
    A. They are looking for eligible partners among Penelope's servant girls.
    B. They are offering their condolences to Penelope on the supposed death of Odysseus.
    C. They are looking to buy Penelope's fine furniture and household items, should she decide to leave the house and move elsewhere.
    D. They are waiting for Penelope to make up her mind which one of them she will marry. While waiting, they are eating and drinking all of the food in the house.

5. What words are used to describe the suitors?
    A. Words like lusty, arrogant, young bloods, and gluttons are used.
    B. The words romantic, handsome, caring, and wise are used.
    C. Words like conceited, mercenary, barbaric, and hateful are used.
    D. The words loving, muscular, cooperative, and nimble are used.

Odyssey Multiple Choice Study Guide Questions Page 2

6. How does Athena present herself to Telemakhos?
    A. She comes in a cloud of light, as befits a goddess.
    B. She come to his home disguised as Mentes, an old friend of his father.
    C. She comes dressed as a beggar woman.
    D. She appears in a dream and looks like his father.

7. Athena tells Telemakhos to seek information about his father, Odysseus, from which men?
    A. He should seek information from Pehmius at Mount Neion, and from Achinalus in Temese.
    B. He should seek information from Nestor in Pylos and Menelaus in Sparta.
    C. He should seek information from Laertes in Rheithron and Samos in Ithaka.
    D. He should seek information from Ilus in Ephyra and Thoosa in Kronos.

8. Athena gives Telemakhos one piece of information about his father. What is it?
    A. She tells him that Odysseus will not be able to return until he has performed twelve feats of daring to appease the gods.
    B. She tells him that Odysseus has lost his memory. If he is able to regain it, he will return home. Otherwise, he will be doomed to wander for his entire life.
    C. She tells him that Odysseus has become overcome by greed and is plundering every place he lands. If he continues to do this, it will take him many more years to reach home.
    D. She tells him that Odysseus is not dead, but is detained somewhere on the seas. She says Odysseus can and will do anything to get home.

9. To whom does Athena refer when she says: "They all would find death was quick, and marriage a painful matter?"
    A. She refers to the young virgins in Ithaka.
    B. She refers to the Trojans.
    C. She refers to the suitors.
    D. She refers to the widows left after the war.

10. What does Athena counsel Telemakhos to do to the suitors?
    A. She suggests giving them huge sums of gold and sending them away.
    B. She suggests killing them either openly or by treachery.
    C. She suggest putting spells on them and having them fall in love with animals.
    D. She suggests introducing them to some of the young maidens from the city in the hopes that they will marry and forget their quest.

Odyssey Multiple Choice Study Guide Questions Page 3

NOTICE lines 296-300 where Athena describes (and praises) the glory given to Orestes. His father was Agamemnon, King of Mykene, who led the Greeks against Troy. (Helen of Troy was rather willingly abducted by Paris. She was married to Menelaus, brother of Agamemnon, king of Sparta.) When Agamemnon came home from Troy, his wife Klytiamnestra and her lover Aigisthos murdered him at the welcoming banquet. When Orestes comes of age, he returns home from Athens and kills Aigisthos. Thus, Athena is telling Telemakhos in her praise of Orestes that a noble son must avenge a wrong committed against a father or a father's house. (Agamemnon tells Odysseus this in Book XI when Odysseus visits Hades. He does not know of Orestes' part, though.)

11. How has Telemakhos changed since the beginning of Book I, and how does Penelope react?
    A. He has become more assertive, referring to himself as the man of the house. She looks at him in wonder.
    B. He has become more child-like and unable to make a decision. Penelope is worried, because he is not able to protect her from the suitors.
    C. He has become quarrelsome and arrogant. Penelope hopes his behavior will drive the suitors away.
    D. He has become disinterested and listless. She is worried that he will waste away.

Odyssey Multiple Choice Study Guide Questions Page 4

Book II

12. Why does Telemakhos call the men to assembly?
    A. He wants to organize a group to search for his father.
    B. He wants to update them on the course of the war.
    C. He wants to offer a sacrifice to the gods.
    D. He wants to publicly address the problem of the suitors.

13. How has Penelope managed to hold off the suitors' demands for the past four years?
    A. She appeals to them to let her finish a death shroud for Laertes, father of Odysseus, so that when he dies she can properly bind him as is her duty (since his wife is dead). She weaves the shroud by day and then unweaves it at night to prolong having to answer to the suitors.
    B. She pretends to be so grief stricken that she cannot function competently. Only one of her maidservants knows the truth.
    C. She demands that they perform tasks so difficult that none of them has been able to succeed.
    D. She deliberately gains a lot of weight and lets the condition of her skin and teeth deteriorate in the hope that if she is unattractive, they will leave her alone.

14. What sign does Zeus send to assembly, and what is its meaning?
    A. He sends a thunderbolt into the crowd. It singes the hair on the beard of one of the men. It means that anyone who crosses Odysseus will be punished.
    B. Zeus launches a pair of eagles who drop on the heads of the crowd (a death omen). Halitherses, who is skilled in reading birdflight, tells them it means that Odysseus is alive and will return soon. When he does, the suitors will be killed.
    C. He causes the sky to turn black in the middle of the day, and a fierce wind comes from the south. This shows the people that they are in disfavor with the god and must make atonement.
    D. He shows an image of a table laden with all kinds of food. This means that a great feast will soon be held.

15. True or False: Telemakhos goes to the armory to sharpen and repair the weapons. Then he begins recruiting men who will help him drive the suitors from his house.
    A. True
    B. False

Odyssey Multiple Choice Study Guide Questions Page 5

Book III

16. Where does the action in Book III take place?
    A. The action takes place at Pylos.
    B. The action takes place in Ithaka.
    C. The action takes place at Lakedaimon.
    D. The action takes place on the isle of Asteris.

17. Where is Athena during this part of the story?
    A. She has returned to Mount Olympos for a meeting with the other Gods.
    B. She has accompanied Telemakhos on his journey, in the disguise of Mentor.
    C. She is with Penelope, disguised as one of the handmaidens.
    D. She is with Odysseus.

18. Who is the friend of Odysseus' who also fought in the Trojan war?
    A. It is Artemis.
    B. It is Taygetos.
    C. It is Nestor.
    D. It is Thyestes.

19. What happens at the homecoming of Agamemnon?
    A. He is honored by the people and sees his new son for the first time.
    B. His family has kept the homecoming a secret so they can greet him privately. He is pleased.
    C. He is murdered by his wife, Klytaimnestra, and her lover, Aigisthos.
    D. Athena appears and praises him for his bravery.

20. What does Orestes do?
    A. He presents Agamemnon with a cloak of golden silk.
    B. He avenges his father's death.
    C. He sacrifices a calf to Athena in his father's name.
    D. He leaves the city because he does not want to see Agamemnon.

21. How does Nestor help Telemakhos?
    A. Nestor offers a sacrifice to the gods in the name of Telemakhos.
    B. Nestor gives Telemakhos a cart and a team of horses to take him on his inland journey.
    C. Nestor accompanies Telemakhos on his journey.
    D. Nestor gives Telemakhos a magic cloak that will carry him speedily over the land. It also makes him invisible whenever anyone else is nearby.

Odyssey Multiple Choice Study Guide Questions Page 6

22. Who accompanies Telemakhos to Sparta to the house of Menelaus?
    A. Peisistratos does.
    B. Diomedes does.
    C. Athena does.
    D. Ortilochus does.

Odyssey Multiple Choice Study Guide Questions Page 7

Book IV
23. True or False: The setting of Book IV is the home of Menelaus in Sparta.
    A. True
    B. False

24. Who first recognizes Telemakhos as the son of Odysseus?
    A. Helen does.
    B. Menelaus does.
    C. Eteoneus does.
    D. Atreus does.

25. Menelaus describes his stay in Egypt to Telemakhos. During his stay there, who tells Menelaus where Odysseus was detained?
    A. Proteus, the Old Man of the Sea, does.
    B. Megapenthes does.
    C. Tyaeus does.
    D. Polyoos does.

26. According to Menelaus' informant, where was Odysseus?
    A. He was on Mount Olympos.
    B. He was being detained on an island by the nymph Kalypso.
    C. He was in the country of Sidon.
    D. He was still in Troy, cleaning up after the war.

27. Why is Menelaus to go to the Elysian Field instead of dying as other mortals do?
    A. His offerings to the gods are so far superior to all of the others that they awarded him that privilege.
    B. It was a promise that Athena made long ago to his mother.
    C. He is to be an inspiration to other mortals, that a valiant and honest life has rewards.
    D. He is the husband of Helen, and son-in-law of Zeus, and he will not die.

28. The scene shifts to the home of Odysseus. What plan do the suitors devise against Telemakhos?
    A. They kidnap Penelope and tell Telemakhos she does not want to see him ever again, hoping that he will commit suicide in his anguish.
    B. They convince two of the maidservants to poison his food a little bit every night for a week so that it will look like he died of a stomach ailment.
    C. They put a ship in the harbor in order to ambush and kill him when he returns.
    D. They sent a messenger to him with bones that supposedly belong to Odysseus. They think if he has evidence of his father's death he will let one of them marry his mother.

Odyssey Multiple Choice Study Guide Questions Page 8

29. Identify the leading men of the suitors.
    A. They are Antinoos and Eurymachos.
    B. They are Phaedimus and Eupeithes.
    C. They are Phrontus and Noemon.
    D. They are Hephaestus and Neleian.

30. Who comforts Penelope after she learns of the suitors plan and the journey of Telemakhos?
    A. Laertes comes from his house in the country and confronts her.
    B. Athena, disguised as Penelope's sister Iphtime, does.
    C. Her maid Euryklela, does.
    D. No one. She has given strict orders that she wants to be alone.

Odyssey Multiple Choice Study Guide Questions Page 9

Book V
31. True or False: Kalypso repents that she has kept Odysseus away from his family so long. She finally realizes that he will never love her. She decides to give him his freedom.
    A. True
    B. False

32. Which god or goddess brings a message from Zeus to Kalypso?
    A. Kadmos, the ship builder's daughter, does.
    B. Nausikaa, daughter of Alkinoos, ruler of Skherta, finds Odysseus.
    C. Leukothea, a sea nymph, finds him.
    D. Hermes does.

33. What happens to Odysseus on the eighteenth day, just as he sights the shores of Skheria?
    A. He is attacked by a great whale who swallows the raft. Odysseus manages to swim to safety.
    B. Poseidon, returning from a vacation in Ethiopia, sees the raft. In a rage he creates a storm which destroys the raft.
    C. He gets a severe sunburn and falls into a feverish coma. When he awakens he doesn't know where he is.
    D. He sees a mirage of a bucket of cool water, created by one of the gods. He is thirsty and drinks most of it, then gets violently ill.

34. What help does Ino give to Odysseus?
    A. She creates a magic ship for him.
    B. She sends a pod of dolphins to surround and protect his ship.
    C. She gives him her magic veil which allows him to survive the long swim to Skheria.
    D. She calms the wind so the waves are not too big.

35. True or False: At the end of Book V, the ocean currents take Odysseus to the mouth of a river. He swims up the river and lands safely on the shore.
    A. True
    B. False

Odyssey Multiple Choice Study Guide Questions Page 10

Book VI

36. Who discovers Odysseus on the shore?
    A. Kadmos, the ship builder's daughter, does.
    B. Nausikaa, daughter of Alkinoos, ruler of Skheria, finds Odysseus.
    C. Leukothea, a sea nymph, finds him.
    D. Amphitrite, his chief maid, does.

37. True or False: This person is near the river because Athena had come to her in a dream and chided her for having soiled clothes. According to Athena, no one will want to marry a girl (regardless of her station in life) who has piles of dirty laundry around. When she awoke in the morning, she gathered the dirty laundry and she and her maids set out for the river to wash the clothes.
    A. True
    B. False

38. What does Odysseus' discoverer do for him?
    A. She gives him another ship and sends him on his way home.
    B. She gives him food and olive oil. Then she guides him to the city and tells him to approach the ruler.
    C. She goes to the temple and makes an offering to Zeus in his name.
    D. She says she will help him if he agrees to marry her.

39. Why doesn't his benefactor bring Odysseus to the palace in person?
    A. She is of marriageable age and does not wish to appear to favor a foreign man when there are noble Phaiakians to choose as a husband. She does not want to cause gossip and resentment among her possible suitors.
    B. She has been banished from the palace for a fortnight for misconduct. If she returns early, she will be beheaded.
    C. She wants to keep his presence a secret, hoping she can keep him for herself.
    D. She is embarrassed to be seen in public in her poor, shabby clothes.

Odyssey Multiple Choice Study Guide Questions Page 11

Book VII

40. Whom does Odysseus approach for assistance when he enters the palace?
- A. Odysseus grasps the knees of Arete, the wife of Alkinoos.
- B. Odysseus approaches Alkinoos.
- C. He approaches Nausikaa.
- D. Odysseus salutes Eurymedon, the chief of the army.

41. What does Alkinoos offer to Odysseus so he could stay with the Phaiakians?
- A. He offers him marriage with Nausikaa.
- B. He offers him half the wealth of the country.
- C. He offers him the best and swiftest ship in the fleet.
- D. He offers him a house and servants and any material goods he wants.

Odyssey Multiple Choice Study Guide Questions Page 12

Book VIII

42. Odysseus is insulted by Seareach. What does he accuse Odysseus of being?
    A. Seareach accuses Odysseus of being a spy who wants to steal the secrets of the Phaikians' seafaring skills.
    B. He accuses Odysseus of being a fortune-hunter who only wants to marry a rich wife and live comfortably on her wealth.
    C. Seareach accuses Odysseus of being a man concerned only with business and profits, and not with being an athlete.
    D. He accuses Odysseus of being a curse sent from the gods to destroy their way of life.

43. With Athena's help, what athletic feat does Odysseus accomplish?
    A. He rows a boat the fastest between two marked points.
    B. He throws a heavy discus the farthest distance.
    C. He wins in a hurdle-jumping contest.
    D. He wins a wrestling match with the Paikian's undefeated champion.

44. Odysseus brags that he is an accomplished athlete but allows one test where the Phaiakians would likely win. To which test does he refer? Why?
    A. He says he would not do well in boxing, since it is not popular among his people.
    B. Odysseus says he would not perform well in archery, since he did not have a bow while on the island with Kalypso and is out of practice.
    C. He says he would not perform well in weight lifting, since he injured his back during the war.
    D. Odysseus says he would not perform well in a foot race, since he has been battered by the sea for so many days.

45. Why do you think Homer interrupts the narrative to have Demodokos sing about the love of Ares and Aphrodite?
    A. Homer wants to remind the readers not to commit immoral actions.
    B. Homer wants to show that the Paiakians are really good hosts.
    C. Homer wants to remind his own listeners that storytellers are blessed by the Muse and should be treated well.
    D. It serves the same purpose as an intermission. People can take a break without losing the story line.

Odyssey Multiple Choice Study Guide Questions Page 13

Book IX

NOTE: In books IX through XII Homer provides us with a flashback to supply background information. He has Odysseus identify himself and tell the Phaikians of his wanderings since he left Troy.

46. Which encounter does Odysseus and his men have before Polyphemos?
    A. They come to the island of Kalypso and leave Odysseus there.
    B. They sack Ismaros and take the Kikones' wives and possessions.
    C. They kill the Kyclopes.
    D. They are shipwrecked on the island of Aeolus.

47. Why is it necessary for Odysseus to take some of his men by force away from the land of the Lotos-Eaters?
    A. The lotos fruit contained a magical drug that made them want to stay and eat more.
    B. The lotos fruit gave them panic attacks. They became fearful of embarking on another sea voyage.
    C. The lotos fruit paralyzed them and they were not able to leave by themselves.
    D. The lotos fruit made them fall in love with the women of the land and not want to leave.

48. True or False: In the next land, Odysseus encounters the Kyklopes, one-eyed giants who are quite lawless.
    A. True
    B. False

49. True or False: Odysseus leads the men into Polyphemos' cave to protect them from the harsh, extremely hot midday sun.
    A. True
    B. False

50. What happens when Polyphemos finds Odysseus and his men in the cave?
    A. He shouts to the others to come and look at the curious creatures he has discovered.
    B. He thinks they are elves sent from the gods. He offers them hospitality.
    C. Polyphemos is quite angry at the intrusion. He scoffs at Odysseus' request for courtesy. Instead, Polyphemos devours two of Odysseus' men.
    D. Polyphemos is not interested in them at all. He does his work and ignores them.

Odyssey Multiple Choice Study Guide Questions Page 14

51. How is Odysseus able to wound Polyphemos?
    A. Odysseus poisons the wine and makes Polyphemos so sick that he is unable to defend himself.
    B. Odysseus and his men use a log sharpened on one end and drive it into his eye while he sleeps.
    C. Odysseus drives his sword through Polyphemos' liver.
    D. Odysseus and his men set Polyphemos on fire while he is milking the goats.

52. How do Odysseus and his remaining men escape from he cave?
    A. They set a brush fire in the cave, then crawl out when the giant pushes away the boulder to let out the smoke.
    B. They find a small opening at the back of the cave and escape through it.
    C. They lash themselves to the bellies of the rams and escape when Polyphemos lets the sheep out in the morning.
    D. They hide in the pockets of his tunic and in his wine skin. When he gets outside the cave, they jump down and run away.

53. How is the craftiness and cunning of Odysseus revealed in this escape?
    A. He allows a few of his men to be sacrificed for the good of the rest.
    B. He makes sure his men are well-fed so they are strong enough to accomplish their tasks.
    C. He brings along the potent wine and he tells Polyphemos that his name is Nobody.
    D. He makes sure to attack only one Kyclopes, when the others are not around to help him.

54. Why does Odysseus reveal his name to Polyphemos after he has escaped?
    A. He wants Polyphemos to warn the other Kyclopes not to try and take revenge.
    B. He wants Polyphemos to make an offering to the gods on his behalf.
    C. He wants Polyphemos to fear the name of Odysseus forever, should he ever return.
    D. He is a hero of the Trojan War and a brave and proud man. He wants Polyphemos to know who bested him.

Odyssey Multiple Choice Study Guide Questions Page 15

Book X

55. What natural phenomenon is controlled by Aeolus?
    A. He controls the tides.
    B. He controls the winds.
    C. He controls the seasons.
    D. He controls the rain.

56. How does the Aeolus show his goodwill when Odysseus is about to leave?
    A. He gives Odysseus a magic bag that contains the current they need to guide them home.
    B. He gives them a star chart and enough food to last a month.
    C. He gives Odysseus a rope with an anchor attached. Whenever the winds die down, they are to throw the rope out over the front of the boat and then pull with all of their strength. Thus they will be able to pull themselves along on the correct course.
    D. He gives Odysseus a bag that contains the destructive storm winds. As long as the bag remains closed, Odysseus will have smooth sailing.

57. Odysseus and his men come within sight of Ithaka. Why do they not land?
    A. They are afraid they will not be remembered and will be killed as intruders.
    B. They want to wait until they have time to clean up and properly prepare themselves.
    C. The men think the bag from Aeolus contains treasure that Odysseus is keeping for himself. While Odysseus is sleeping, they open the bag. The winds escape and they are blown back to the Aeolan island.
    D. The ship is sunk on a reef.

58. Odysseus asks for further help from Aeolus. What is his reply?
    A. Aeolus believes the gods hate Odysseus and that is why he has been blown back to the island. He refuses to help anyone who is in disfavor with the gods.
    B. Aeolus says his magic will work only once, but Odysseus is welcome to stay there and live out his days.
    C. Aeolus doesn't recognize Odysseus and turns him away.
    D. Aeolus gladly agrees to help again.

59. Describe the Laestrygonians.
    A. They are delicate and as lovely as the gods.
    B. They are uglier than any other creatures on earth.
    C. They are half human, half lion.
    D. They are giants and cannibals.

Odyssey Multiple Choice Study Guide Questions Page 16

60. Who helps Odysseus outwit Kirke?
   A. Athena does.
   B. Helios does.
   C. Ares does.
   D. Hermes does.

61. Why must Odysseus visit the house of Hades?
   A. He has to get magical supplies for his ship, and Hades is the only place to get them.
   B. He must consult with the blind prophet Teiresias, who will tell Odysseus all he needs to know about getting home.
   C. He must atone for his past misbehavior before he can go home.
   D. He has to deliver the dead crewmen.

Odyssey Multiple Choice Study Guide Questions Page 17

Book XI

62. How does Odysseus gain access to the underworld?
   A. Odysseus follows Kirke's instructions and digs a votive pit. He pours libations to the dead and sacrifices the lamb and ewe given him by Kirke.
   B. He steers the ship near a whirlpool, then jumps into the sea. The whirlpool sucks him down into Hades.
   C. He cuts the vein on his right forearm and lets the blood flow over a special stone given him by Athena. The stone turns into a cave, which he enters, and walks through to Hades.
   D. He drinks a magic potion that makes him fall into a trance. The spirits come and transport him to Hades, then return him to the ship when his business is completed.

63. What does Odysseus promise Elpenor?
   A. He promises to return to Kirke's island and bury Elpenor's body.
   B. He promises to tell of Elpenor's brave deeds wherever he tells the story of his own adventures.
   C. He promises to take care of Elpenor's wife and children.
   D. He promises to avenge Elpenor's death.

64. Why does Odysseus not let his mother come near the blood?
   A. He is afraid she will haunt him.
   B. He does not recognize her because she was alive when he left Ithaka for the war.
   C. He is waiting for Teiresias to speak to him first.
   D. He does not want to scare her. He knows she always hated the sight of blood.

65. Which of the following is not one of the things Teiresias tells Odysseus?
   A. He must perform ten good works before he can go home.
   B. He tells him that his homecoming will be a hard one.
   C. He gives Odysseus a warning not to harm the sheep and cattle of Helios on the island of Thrinakia.
   D. He tells Odysseus that when he has put his home in order he must set out again on a journey and find a land where people do not know of the sea or the use of an oar, and there he must make generous sacrifices to Poseidon.

66. Who comes to speak to Odysseus after all the souls of the women have departed?
   A. Salmoneus does.
   B. Neleus does.
   C. Eucheneus does.
   D. Agamemnon does.

Odyssey Multiple Choice Study Guide Questions Page 18

67. What does this person tell Odysseus?
    A. He tells Odysseus all of the events that have happened in Ithaka since he left.
    B. He tells Odysseus what the future will be like.
    C. He describes his own death in great detail.
    D. He suggests ways to appease the wrath of Poseidon once and for all.

68. Which of the other spirits who speaks to Odysseus is tortured by having an abundance of food and water always just beyond his grasp, so that he constantly starved?
    A. It is Aias.
    B. It is Minos
    C. It is Tantalos.
    D. It is Heracles.

69. True or False: Sisyphos must constantly push a large boulder up a steep hill. As soon as the boulder reaches the top of the hill, the gods send it rolling down, and he must start his labors all over again.
    A. True
    B. False

Odyssey Multiple Choice Study Guide Questions Page 19

Book XII

70. How do Odysseus and his men avoid destruction by the Seirines?
    A. Odysseus orders his men to plug their ears with beeswax and has them lash him to the mast.
    B. They sing their own songs in the loudest possible voices, to drown out the sound of the Seirines.
    C. Athena puts all of the men into a magical sleep and guides the boat through herself.
    D. They throw trinkets and pieces of brightly colored cloth onto the island. The Seirines are fascinated with these items and forget to sing.

71. What are Skylla and Kharybdis?
    A. They are radiant nymphs with beautiful braids. They watch over the cattle and sheep on Thrinacia.
    B. They are two horrible monsters who destroy men as they sail through the narrow straight between them. Skylla has six heads with which she snatches up men from their ships and eats them. Kharybdis is a whirlpool that sucks down men and ships, destroying them.
    C. They are the daughters of Kirke. They have been sent to seduce Odysseus and his men and to return them to her island.
    D. They are the servants of Helios who greet Odysseus when he arrives. Skylla has the power to predict the future. Kharybdis can heal old physical wounds and make people forget old feuds.

72. What happens to Odysseus' companions?
    A. They get curious about the Seirines and return to their island, where they remain forever.
    B. They are destroyed by Zeus because they harm the sheep and cattle of Helios.
    C. They see a comfortable life right where they are and decide to stay.
    D. They grow tired of his misfortunes and leave him to find their own way back to Ithaka.

73. True or False: Odysseus next sets a course for Kalypso's island. He has heard of her beauty and grace and wishes to visit her before he goes home.
    A. True
    B. False

Odyssey Multiple Choice Study Guide Questions Page 20

Book XIII

74. How does Poseidon react when he discovers that the Phaiakians have aided Odysseus in reaching Ithaka?
    A. Poseidon is angry that Odysseus has reached Ithaka easily and with great presents. He punishes the Phaiakians by turning their ship to stone just as it reaches their harbor. He then erects a ring of high mountains around the island, cutting them off from their livelihood.
    B. He grudgingly accepts that they have done a good deed. He causes storms for a few days to let them know he is annoyed, but then leaves them alone.
    C. He tells Zeus to punish Odysseus for not holding the gods in enough reverence.
    D. He just gives up and grudgingly applauds Odysseus' courage.

75. True or False: Odysseus does not recognize his homeland. He thinks the Phaiakians have left him on an undisclosed shore. It is not until he meets Athena, disguised as a swineherd, that he discovers he is, indeed, home.
    A. True
    B. False

76. Why does Athena now reveal herself to Odysseus?
    A. She wants to help him plan his revenge on Penelope's suitors.
    B. She wants him to know she has protected him so he can offer sacrifice to her.
    C. She is angry at Poseidon and wants to antagonize him.
    D. Zeus ordered her to do so because Odysseus was attributing all of his success to his own strength and cunning and not to the help of the gods.

77. Where does Athena send Odysseus first?
    A. She sends him to the harbor to see his ships.
    B. She sends him disguised as a beggar to his loyal swineherd.
    C. She sends him to her altar to make a sacrifice.
    D. She sends him directly to his wife.

78. What task does Athena first set out to do?
    A. She goes to Lakedaimon to bring Telemakhos home.
    B. She goes to Hades to rescue the men Odysseus lost on his journeys.
    C. She goes to the spring at Arethusa to get the magic water.
    D. She goes to Olympos to implore Zeus to give Odysseus good fortune.

Odyssey Multiple Choice Study Guide Questions Page 21

Book XIV

79. Who is Eumaios?
    A. He is Telemakhos' guard.
    B. He is the current ruler of Ithaka
    C. He is Odysseus' faithful swineherd.
    D. He is the elderly scribe who knows all the news of Ithaka.

80. Why does Odysseus hide his identity from Eumaios?
    A. He is afraid the surprise will kill the man.
    B. He has promised Athena he will not reveal his identity yet.
    C. He wants to test Eumaios' loyalty.
    D. He knows the other man likes jokes, so he is just playing a joke on him.

81. Does Eumaois believe Odysseus' tale?
    A. No, he doesn't believe any of it.
    B. Yes, he believes all of it.
    C. Eumaios believes all but the part about Odysseus still being alive.
    D. At first he believes it, but then he sees an omen that he thinks means the tale is false.

Odyssey Multiple Choice Study Guide Questions Page 22

Book XV

82. Telemakhos receives an omen as he is about to depart. What is it, and what does it mean?
    A. Three dark clouds travel across the sun. Those who see it think it means that something terrible will happen in three days.
    B. He sees a double rainbow over the bow of the ship. He thinks it is a good luck sign, that he will have a safe journey.
    C. A mountain eagle holding a white goose in its talons flies to the right over the horses. Helen interprets the sign to mean that Odysseus will soon return to Ithaka and take revenge on the suitors.
    D. A pod of dolphins surround the ship. The crew thinks this means that they are at last in Poseidon's good graces.

83. Who journeys to Ithaka with Telemakhos and his companions?
    A. Theoklymenos, a gifted prophet and a fugitive from Argos, joins them.
    B. Mesaulius, his loyal servant, travels with him. He has traveled with Telemakhos since Telemakhos was a young boy.
    C. Athena, disguised as the ship's masthead, travels with them.
    D. His friend Orsilochus travels with him. He has pledged to help Telemakhos fight the suitors.

84. Odysseus has a plan that he shares with Eumaios. What is it?
    A. Odysseus will dress in his finest clothing and boldly enter his house.
    B. He will disguise himself as a suitor and try to win Penelope himself.
    C. Odysseus plans to go to his own house and ask for a job as a servant for the suitors.
    D. He will go to town and talk to the families of the suitors and ask them to remove the suitors from his house.

85. What is Eumaios' reaction to Odysseus' idea?
    A. He approves.
    B. He disapproves.

86. How did Eumaios come to be swineherd for Odysseus?
    A. He washed ashore on Ithaka after a shipwreck. He had lost his memory, and had nowhere to go, so he stayed.
    B. His mother was Penelope's servant. She asked that he get the job.
    C. Hermes sent him there to protect him from men in his homeland who wanted to kill him.
    D. He was kidnapped by his nurse and a group of Phoinikian traders who sold him to Laertes.

Odyssey Multiple Choice Study Guide Questions Page 23

87. Which are the two signs that the gods send to Telemakhos and Odysseus?
    A. Telemakhos has a dream about Odysseus and Odysseus has a dream about Telemakhos.
    B. An eagle carrying a white goose flies past Telemakhos on the right side and a falcon carrying a pigeon flies past Odysseus on the right side.
    C. Telemakhos receives a gift of a rare variety of figs and Odysseus receives a bronze-tipped sword. Neither knows who the giver is.
    D. Telemakhos is the only one who can see a rainbow in the sky after a particular storm, and Odysseus can see Penelope even though she can't see him.

Odyssey Multiple Choice Study Guide Questions Page 24

Book XVI

88. What action does Odysseus take?
   A. He offers a ram and ewe in sacrifice to Zeus.
   B. He reveals his true identity to Telemakhos.
   C. He kills two of the suitors who are out for a walk.
   D. He sharpens his sword and does exercises to strengthen himself.

89. What instructions does Odysseus give to Telemakhos?
   A. He tells him to take Penelope away into a special hiding place in the woods and wait for a signal when it will be safe to come back. He says not to tell anyone else of the hiding place and to make sure they are not followed.
   B. He tells him to go home and act like a madman and threaten the suitors. Then he should lock himself and Penelope in her quarters and send his servant to Odysseus when this has been accomplished.
   C. He tells him to go home and wait for his father's arrival as a beggar. He warns Telemakhos not to interfere if the suitors are rude, but to wait for the signal to hide all weapons except their own. He also reminds Telemakhos not to let anyone know that he (Odysseus) has returned.
   D. He tells Telemakhos to go to the house disguised as another suitor. He should try to get the others into jealous quarrels and keep them distracted.

Odyssey Multiple Choice Study Guide Questions Page 25

Book XVII

90. Penelope greets Telemakhos when he arrives home and asks to hear his news. Does he tell her the truth?
    A. Yes, he does.
    B. No, he does not.

91. Identify the speaker: "See now how the rascal comes on leading a rascal about: like guides what is like itself, just as a god does."
    A. This is spoken by Peisistratus, son of Nestor, to Telemakhos upon his departure.
    B. This is spoken by Theaclmenus in greeting to Telemakhos.
    C. It is spoken by Melanthios, disloyal goatherd of Odysseus, to Eumaios and Odysseus.
    D. It is spoken by Eurymachos, the most ardent suitor, to Penelope's maidservants.

92. What two physical assaults does Odysseus endure?
    A. First he is stabbed by Eurymachos and then he is thrown into the fountain by Argos.
    B. First he is kicked by Melanthios at the fountain and then he is hit with a footstool thrown by Antinoos in his own house.
    C. First he is punched and kicked by Antinoos and then his clothes are torn by Eupeithes.
    D. First he is bitten by his own dog and then he is pushed down the stairs by Phemius.

93. True or False: Argus is Odysseus' beloved hunting dog. He recognizes Odysseus, disguised as a beggar, when Odysseus and Eumaios approach the house. He is old, and now dies, happy that he has seen his master one last time.
    A. True
    B. False

Odyssey Multiple Choice Study Guide Questions Page 26

Book XVIII

94. What occurs between Odysseus and Iros? Why?
   A. They have a debate on who the most promising suitor is.
   B. They have a fist fight to decide which beggar may stay and which may leave.
   C. Iros thinks he recognizes the beggar as Odysseus. Odysseus has to deny it and distract Iros by talking about food and women.
   D. They plot together to rob Penelope's house and blame it on the suitors.

95. What reward does Odysseus (still disguised) give to Amphinomos for helping him?
   A. He gives Amphinomos the best pieces of meat from the dinner platter.
   B. Odysseus, while concealing his true identity, warns Amphinomos of the fate awaiting the suitors.
   C. He gives him a sword from Odysseus' storeroom.
   D. Odysseus tells Amphinomos who will be chosen by Penelope.

96. What does Penelope do that makes Odysseus happy?
   A. She refuses to see the suitors and banishes all of them to the courtyard.
   B. She tells the suitors she will never marry again, even if Odysseus is dead.
   C. She offers sacrifice to the gods and prays for her husband's safe return.
   D. She enriches the house by requesting expensive gifts from the suitors.

97. How does Odysseus come to be a target for the footstool again?
   A. Iros is angry at being ridiculed and throws it at him.
   B. He is eating too much of the meal. Antinoos throws it to remind Odysseus (the beggar) of his proper place.
   C. Odysseus insults Eurymachos, and Eurymachos throws the stool in retaliation.
   D. Odysseus takes a seat near the fire. Amphinomous demands the seat. When Odysseus refuses, Amphinomus throws the stool at him.

Odyssey Multiple Choice Study Guide Questions Page 27

Book XIX

98. What action does Odysseus take now?
    A. He and Telemakhos remove the weapons from the hall.
    B. He drugs the wine so the suitors will fall asleep.
    C. He sharpens his sword.
    D. He takes a nap so that he will be rested for the slaughter of the suitors.

99. How does Eurykleia discover the identity of Odysseus?
    A. She recognizes his voice.
    B. She sees a birthmark on his arm.
    C. He smiles and she notices his straight teeth and the cleft in his chin when he smiles.
    D. She recognizes a scar on his leg when she washes his feet.

100. What contest does Penelope devise to test the suitors?
    A. She says she will marry the man who wins against all of the others in a sword fight to the death.
    B. She decides whoever can string the great bow of Odysseus and send an arrow through the iron of twelve axes shall be her husband.
    C. She tells them that whoever is able to move her husband's bed shall be her husband.
    D. She says she will marry the man who will give her her weight in gold.

Odyssey Multiple Choice Study Guide Questions Page 28

Book XX

101. Who tells Odysseus (the beggar) that if Odysseus were to return he would help to destroy the suitors?
    A. Philoitios the cowherd does.
    B. Eurynome does.
    C. Iros the beggar does.
    D. Peisenor's son, Ops, does.

102. While the suitors are plotting Telemakhos' death they see an omen. What is it, and what does it mean?
    A. They see an eagle with a dove in its claws crossing their path from the left. Amphinomos says the sign means that their plan will not work.
    B. They see a stream of muddy water that suddenly rushes through the great hall. Antinoos thinks it means they will soon be sent away.
    C. They see two stars shining brightly in the night sky. They think it means that Penelope will soon choose one of them.
    D. They hear a wolf howling in the distance and take it as a sign that Odysseus is dead.

103. Who warns that evil will come to the suitors before he leaves the house?
    A. Iros does.
    B. Peiraeus does.
    C. Theoklymenos does.
    D. Ktesippos does.

Book XXI

104. Who, other than Odysseus, has the strength and power to string the bow?
    A. Antinoos does.
    B. Telemakhos does.
    C. Laertes does.
    D. Penelope does, because Odysseus taught her.

105. To what men does Odysseus reveal his identity:
    A. He reveals his identity to Telemakhos and Eurymachos.
    B. He reveals his identity to Antinoos and Lapoithae.
    C. He reveals his identity to Eumaios and Philoitios.
    D. He reveals his identity to Laertes and Polybus.

106. True or False: Odysseus plans to set a fire in the great hall and block off the escape routes, making it look like the suitors died by accident.
    A. True
    B. False

Odyssey Multiple Choice Study Guide Questions Page 29

BOOK XXII

107. Which men does Odysseus spare from the slaughter?
    A. He spares Phemios, the minstrel, and Medon, the herald.
    B. He spares Damastor and Demoptolemus, two servants.
    C. He spares Iros and Eurymachos.
    D. He spares Antinoos and Agelaus so that he can torture them at his leisure.

108. What happens to the disloyal serving women?
    A. They are beheaded as adulterers and banished from the city.
    B. They are taken to the sea and set adrift in a boat.
    C. Telemakhos takes them outside, after they have cleared and cleaned the house of their dead lovers. He ties them up against the round house and with a rope hangs all of them.
    D. Odysseus takes pity on them. He returns them to their families and makes them take vows of celibacy.

Book XXIII

109. Why is Penelope so hesitant to greet her husband?
    A. She is no longer sure she really loves him.
    B. She has grown accustomed to living alone and is not sure she wants to resume her married life.
    C. She fears it is a trick or a device of the gods. She wants to be sure it is really Odysseus.
    D. She wants to make sure he is finished with his rage and will not hurt her.

110. How does Penelope test Odysseus?
    A. She asks for details of their wedding and the birth of Telemakhos.
    B. She tells the servants to bring out his bed and then waits for his reaction.
    C. She asks him to name all of her relatives.
    D. She has Eurycleia identify him and then inspects the scar on his leg herself.

Odyssey Multiple Choice Study Guide Questions Page 30

Book XXIV

111. Where does Odysseus go next?
    A. He goes to the temple to make a sacrifice.
    B. He goes to see his ships.
    C. He goes to the home of Laertes.
    D. He takes a walk around his house and grounds.

112. Why does Laertes wear rags and not bathe?
    A. He is despondent that he will never see his son again.
    B. He has lost all of his land and his money.
    C. He thinks that if he suffers enough the gods will take pity and send Odysseus home.
    D. He has no one to care for him since his wife died.

113. What does Athena do when the families of the dead suitors attack Odysseus?
    A. She kills all of the male relatives of the suitors.
    B. She makes Odysseus give gifts to the families of the suitors.
    C. She makes both sides pledge peace.
    D. She puts a protective mist around Odysseus so his enemies can't hurt him.

114. In the oral epic there is a lot of repetition. Which of the following lines is not repeated several times?
    A. "When they had put aside their desire for eating and drinking"
    B. "Blue-eyed, golden capped goddess"
    C. "But when the young Dawn showed again with her rosy fingers."
    D. "They would all find death was quick and marriage a painful matter."

MULTIPLE CHOICE STUDY/QUIZ QUESTIONS ANSWER KEY
ODYSSEY

Book 1	Book II	Book III	Book IV	Book V	Book VI
1 A	12 D	16 A	23 A	31 B	36 B
2 B	13 A	17 B	24 A	32 D	37 A
3 A	14 B	18 C	25 A	33 B	38 B
4 D	15 B	19 C	26 B	34 C	39 A
5 A		20 B	27 D	35 A	
6 B		21 B	28 C		
7 B		22 A	29 A		
8 D			30 B		
9 C					
10 B					
11 A					

Book VII	Book VIII	Book IX	Book X	Book XI	Book XII
40 A	42 C	46 B	55 B	62 A	70 A
41 A	43 B	47 A	56 D	63 A	71 B
	44 D	48 A	57 C	64 C	72 B
	45 C	49 B	58 A	65 A	73 B
		50 C	59 D	66 D	
		51 B	60 D	67 C	
		52 C	61 B	68 C	
		53 C		69 A	
		54 D			

Book XIII	Book XIV	Book XV	Book XVI	Book XVII	Book XVIII
74 A	79 C	82 C	88 B	90 B	94 B
75 A	80 C	83 A	89 C	91 C	95 B
76 A	81 C	84 C		92 B	96 D
77 B		85 B		93 A	97 C
78 A		86 D			
		87 B			

Book XIX	Book XX	Book XXI	Book XXII	Book XXIII	Book XXIV
98 A	101 A	104 B	107 A	109 C	111 C
99 D	102 A	105 C	108 C	110 B	112 A
100 B	103 C	106 B			113 C
					114 B

PREREADING VOCABULARY WORKSHEETS

VOCABULARY - *The Odyssey*

Part I: Using Prior Knowledge and Contextual Clues

Below are the sentences in which the vocabulary words appear in the text. Read the sentence. Use any clues you can find in the sentence combined with your prior knowledge, and write what you think the underlined words mean in the space provided.

Books I and II

1. "...tell the story of that man skilled in all ways of contending"

2. "...after he plundered the stronghold on the proud height of Troy"

3. "...that point of time ordained for him to make his voyage home..."

4. "But not by will nor by valor could he save them..."

5. "...I should take steps to make these men disperse."

6. "...He found the criers with clarion voices..."

7. "...and no one had the audacity to answer harshly..."

8. "They(the eagles) wheeled,...wielding their talons, tearing cheeks and throats..."

9. "...and he, the great tactician, joined the rest."

10. "..The double doors were...guarded by Peisinor, in all her duty vigilant and shrewd."

Odyssey Vocabulary Worksheet Books 1-II Continued

Part II: Determining the Meaning
　　Match the vocabulary words to their dictionary definitions.

  ___ 1. contending　　　　　A. prearranged, predestined
  ___ 2. plundered　　　　　　B. scattered in various directions
  ___ 3. ordained　　　　　　　C. handling a weapon or tool
  ___ 4. valor　　　　　　　　　D. boldness or daring
  ___ 5. dispersed　　　　　　E. striving in battle or controversy
  ___ 6. clarion　　　　　　　　F. watchfulness
  ___ 7. audacity　　　　　　　G. courage and boldness
  ___ 8. wielding　　　　　　　H. a person skilled in maneuvering
  ___ 9. tactician　　　　　　　I. shrill and clear
  ___ 10. vigilance　　　　　　J. robbed of goods by force

Odyssey-Vocabulary Worksheet Books III - IV

Part I: Using Prior Knowledge and Contextual Clues
    Below are the sentences in which the vocabulary words appear in the text. Read the sentence. Use any clues you can find in the sentence combined with your prior knowledge, and write what you think the underlined words mean in the space provided.

1. "Athena liked...the equity that gave her precedence with the cup of gold."

2. "Are you reckless wanderers of the sea, like those corsairs?"

3. "Menelaus harangued them to get organized."

4. "I'd be revenged on my insidious and brazen enemies"

5. "The others made libation, and drank deep."

6. "No mortal man can vie with Zeus."

7. "They were drinking an anodyne, mild magic of forgetfulness."

8. "These valors could not defend him from annihilation."

9. "You know the reason-why feign not to know?"

10. "Poseidon landed him on Gyrai promontory."

Odyssey-Vocabulary Worksheet Books III - IV Continued

Part II: Determining the Meaning
Match the vocabulary words to their dictionary definitions.

___ 1. precedence
___ 2. corsairs
___ 3. harangued
___ 4. insidious
___ 5. libation
___ 6. vie
___ 7. anodyne
___ 8. annihilation
___ 9. feign
___ 10. promontory

A. working or spreading harmfully in a sly way
B. to compete or strive for victory
C. the act of destroying completely
D. pirates
E. a high ridge of land or rock jutting into the sea
F. priority: going in advance
G. to pretend
H. anything that soothes or confronts
I. pouring a liquid offered as a religious ritual
J. delivered a long strong-feeling speech

Odyssey-Vocabulary Worksheet Books V - VI

Part I: Using Prior Knowledge and Contextual Clues
    Below are the sentences in which the vocabulary words appear in the text. Read the sentence. Use any clues you can find in the sentence combined with your prior knowledge, and write what you think the underlined words mean in the space provided.

Books V and VI

1. "A gull patrolling between the wave crests of the desolate sea will dip.."

2. "A deep wood grew outside, with...pungent cypress."

3. "...food and drink for the luminous Wayfinder"

4. "She had to give him...a well-polished adze."

5. "But in perplexity Od said to himself, his great heart laboring:"

6. "Far gone in weariness, in oblivion, the noble man slept on."

7. "...and twirling out of her distaff yarn dyed like the sea..."

8. "But one man's destiny is more than blest-he who prevails and takes you as his bride."

9. "I hold it shame for any girl to flout her own dear parents."

10. "In deference to her father's brother she would not show her true form."

Odyssey-Vocabulary Worksheet Books V - VI Continued

Part II: Determining the Meaning
Match the vocabulary words to their dictionary definitions.

___ 1. desolate
___ 2. pungent
___ 3. luminous
___ 4. adze
___ 5. perplexity
___ 6. oblivion
___ 7. distaff
___ 8. prevails
___ 9. flout
___ 10. deference

A. emitting self-generated light
B. the state of being puzzled or confused
C. a stick on a spinning wheel that holds unspun wool
D. courteous respect
E. triumphs or wins, becomes effective
F. a sharp, bitter taste
G. the state of being completely forgotten
H. to show contempt or scorn
I. an axe-like tool with an arched blade at right angles to the handle
J. deserted: dreary, gloomy

Odyssey-Vocabulary Worksheet Books VII - VIII

Part I: Using Prior Knowledge and Contextual Clues
    Below are the sentences in which the vocabulary words appear in the text. Read the sentence. Use any clues you can find in the sentence combined with your prior knowledge, and write what you think the underlined words mean in the space provided.

1. "...so I turned back and came to a river, to <u>auspicious</u> water..."

2. "...a kingly bed, with purple rugs..and fleecy coverlets in an eastern <u>colonnade</u>."

3. "...learn about the stranger...a <u>comely</u> man: the gods' own light is on him."

4. "She put him in a <u>fettle</u> to win the day."

5. "Neck like a <u>bollard</u>, strong as a bull he seems."

6. "Od, the <u>canniest</u> of men, replied:"

7. "Now Seareach put his word, and <u>contentiously</u>:"

8. "You'd have us note the <u>prowess</u> that is in you."

9. "We have our skills...not in the boxing ring nor the <u>palestra</u> conspicuous..."

10. "They sat nearby with long drawn out and <u>hapless</u> argument.

Odyssey-Vocabulary Worksheet Books VII - VIII Continued

Part II: Determining the Meaning
  Match the vocabulary words to their dictionary definitions.

___ 1. auspicious   A. a thick post on ship, used for securing ropes
___ 2. colonnade   B. attended to by favorable circumstances
___ 3. comely   C. quarrelsome
___ 4. fettle   D. a public place for training and practicing athletics
___ 5. bollard   E. a series of column placed at regular intervals
___ 6. canniest   F. luckless, unfortunate
___ 7. contentiously   G. proper or sound condition; good spirits
___ 8. prowess   H. superior skill or ability
___ 9. palestra   I. shrewd; attentive to all factors
___ 10. hapless   J. attractive, handsome, graceful

Odyssey-Vocabulary Worksheet Book IX

Part I: Using Prior Knowledge and Contextual Clues
　　　Below are the sentences in which the vocabulary words appear in the text. Read the sentence. Use any clues you can find in the sentence combined with your prior knowledge, and write what you think the underlined words mean in the space provided.

1. "I am Odysseus, formidable for guile in peace and war."

2. "My men were mutinous, fools, on stores of wine."

3. "Kyklopes have no muster and no meeting."

4. "...vines in profusion, prairie, clear for the plow..."

5. "A prodigious man slept in this cave alone."

6. "...the sweet scent hovered like a fume over the wine bowl..."

7. "We cried aloud,...looking on at this, appalled; powerless."

8. "He caught another brace of men."

9. "...but my men riding on the pectoral fleece..."

10. "...he'll get the range and lob a boulder..."

Odyssey-Vocabulary Worksheet Book IX

Part II: Determining the Meaning
Match the vocabulary words to their dictionary definitions.

___ 1. guile
___ 2. mutinous
___ 3. muster
___ 4. profusion
___ 5. prodigious
___ 6. hovered
___ 7. appalled
___ 8. brace
___ 9. lob

A. to hit, toss, or propel in a high arc
B. impressively great in size
C. rebellious
D. abundance, extravagance
E. a pair of things
F. filled with dismay
G. to assemble or gather
H. treacherous cunning, craftiness
I. floated as if suspended

Odyssey-Vocabulary Worksheet Books X - XII

Part I: Using Prior Knowledge and Contextual Clues

    Below are the sentences in which the vocabulary words appear in the text. Read the sentence. Use any clues you can find in the sentence combined with your prior knowledge, and write what you think the underlined words mean in the space provided.

1. When I asked provisioning he stinted nothing.

2. "... they met a stalwart young girl taking her pail to Artakia."

3. "But he put both hands around my knees and said in supplications..."

4. "...But when it passed his lips he had succumbed..."

5. "...you would not forget...your fury with me over those accurst calamitous arms?..."

6. "...gorgeous intaglio of savage bears, boars, lions..."

7. "Persephone had brought from darker hell some saurian death's head"

8. "No birds can pass them by, not even the timorous doves..."

9. "They came up around the wreck, bobbing like petrels on the waves."

Odyssey-Vocabulary Worksheet Books X - XII Continued

Part II: Determining the Meaning
   Match the vocabulary words to their dictionary definitions.

___ 1. stinted
___ 2. stalwart
___ 3. supplication
___ 4. succumbed
___ 5. calamitous
___ 6. intaglio
___ 7. saurian
___ 8. timorous
___ 9. petrels

A. asking for humbly or earnestly
B. restricted or limited
C. yielded or submitted to an overpowering force
D. a design incised beneath the surface of metal
E. any of an order of sea birds
F. full of apprehensiveness
G. causing or involving a disaster
H. lizard-like
I. having physical strength

Odyssey-Vocabulary Worksheet Books XIII - XIV

Part I: Using Prior Knowledge and Contextual Clues
   Below are the sentences in which the vocabulary words appear in the text. Read the sentence. Use any clues you can find in the sentence combined with your prior knowledge, and write what you think the underlined words mean in the space provided.

1. "Only Odysseus turned craning toward the sun.

2. "...But there is nothing meager about the soil..."

3. "...even a god might bow to you in ways of dissimulation..."

4. "We go to make a cache now."

5. "Now then, their colloquy at an end, they went their ways."

6. "This time you are the derelict the Powers bring."

7. "On this he rose and placed the bed of balsam near the fire."

Part II: Determining the Meaning
   Match the vocabulary words to their dictionary definitions

   ___ 1. craning   A. to conceal or disguises
   ___ 2. meager   B. a hole or hiding place
   ___ 3. dissimulation   C. a tree that yields an aromatic, sticky substance
   ___ 4. cache   D. stretching and straining
   ___ 5. colloquy   E. a vagrant or social outcast
   ___ 6. derelict   F. a formal conversation
   ___ 7. balsam   G. deficient in quality, fullness, or extent

Odyssey-Vocabulary Worksheet Books XV - XVI

Part I: Using Prior Knowledge and Contextual Clues
   Below are the sentences in which the vocabulary words appear in the text. Read the sentence. Use any clues you can find in the sentence combined with your prior knowledge, and write what you think the underlined words mean in the space provided.

1. "Check him, or he will have your lands and chattels in spite of you."

2. "Homage to Nestor, the benevolent king."

3. "...hoist aloft the white sail in its halyards."

4. "These are their minions, while their tables gleam and groan under big roasts."

5. "...stone dead she dropped into the sloshing bilge...

6. "Telemakhos with his clear candor said..."

7. "There is no rancor in the town against me."

8. "Our own island accounts for twelve, high-ranked, and their retainers."

9. "...She...spoke directly to Antinoos: "Infatuate, steeped in evil!"

10. "I saw a ship...and I surmised those were the men."

Odyssey-Vocabulary Worksheet Books XV - XVI Continued

Part II: Determining the Meaning
Match the vocabulary words the their dictionary definitions

___ 1. chattels
___ 2. benevolent
___ 3. halyards
___ 4. minions
___ 5. bilge
___ 6. candor
___ 7. rancor
___ 8. retainer
___ 9. steeped
___ 10. surmised

A. subordinates of an organization or an individual
B. frankness, sincerity
C. kind
D. inferred without conclusive evidence
E. an employee or domestic servant
F. soaked
G. articles of personal, movable property; slaves
H. bitter, long-lasting resentment
I. water that collects in the low part of a ship's hull
J. ropes used to raise or lower a sail or flag

Odyssey-Vocabulary Worksheet Book XVII

Part I: Using Prior Knowledge and Contextual Clues

    Below are the sentences in which the vocabulary words appear in the text. Read the sentence. Use any clues you can find in the sentence combined with your prior knowledge, and write what you think the underlined words mean in the space provided.

1. "Some householder may want to dole him out a loaf and a pint."

2. "But as for blows and missiles, I am no tyro at these things."

3. "Say one of our suitors...kill me... and parcel out my patrimony."

4. "Eumaios crossed the court and went straight forward into the megaron and the suitors."

5. "But now the rest of the crowd were mortified..."

6. "...and someone spoke from the crowd to rebuke him."

7. "These had their joy of dance and song as day waned into evening."

Part II: Determining the Meaning

    Match the vocabulary words to their dictionary definitions

    ___ 1. dole   A. a beginner or inexperienced person
    ___ 2. tyro   B. a large room
    ___ 3. patrimony   C. shamed or humiliated
    ___ 4. megaron   D. criticized or reproved sharply
    ___ 5. mortified   E. approaching an end
    ___ 6. rebuke   F. an inheritance from a father
    ___ 7. waned   G. to distribute in small portions

Odyssey-Vocabulary Worksheet Books XVIII - XX

Part I: Using Prior Knowledge and Contextual Clues
    Below are the sentences in which the vocabulary words appear in the text. Read the sentence. Use any clues you can find in the sentence combined with your prior knowledge, and write what you think the underlined words mean in the space provided.

1. "Patience: a windfall from the gods will come."

2. "What a farce heaven has brought this house."

3. "...a wide, resplendent robe, fastened with twelve brooches..."

4. "Yet the girl felt nothing for her mistress, no compunction."

5. "You'd see then if I cleft you in a straight furrow."

6. "Mistress, mend your ways, or you may lose all the vivacity of yours."

7. "...let someone in the waking house give me good augury..."

8. "...and twelve maids had the job of grinding out whole grain, the pith of men."

9. "You could not be reproached for obstinacy."

Odyssey-Vocabulary Worksheet Books XVIII - XX Continued

Part II: Determining the Meaning
  Match the vocabulary words to their dictionary definitions

____ 1. windfall   A. strong uneasiness caused by a sense of guilt
____ 2. farce   B. liveliness
____ 3. resplendent   C. the essential or central part of anything
____ 4. compunction   D. a sudden and unexpected piece of good fortune
____ 5. cleft   E. brilliant
____ 6. vivacity   F. interpreting signs and omens
____ 7. augury   G. stubbornness
____ 8. pith   H. empty show; mockery
____ 9. obstinacy   I. divided, split, separated

Odyssey-Vocabulary Worksheet Books XXI - XXII

Part I: Using Prior Knowledge and Contextual Clues
　　Below are the sentences in which the vocabulary words appear in the text. Read the sentence. Use any clues you can find in the sentence combined with your prior knowledge, and write what you think the underlined words mean in the space provided.

1. "Then came a...bellow like a bull's vaunt in a meadow."

2. "A taut cord aligned the socket rings."

3. "Are you not coddled here enough?"

4. "Friends," he said, "the man is implacable."

5. "They stood four at the entry, facing two score men."

6. "...Still others rand on the stone wall, shivering hafts of ash."

7. "He tied one end of a hawser to a pillar."

Part II: Determining the Meaning
　　Match the vocabulary words to their dictionary definitions

___ 1. vaunt		A. treated indulgently; babied
___ 2. taut		B. a cable or rope used in mooring a ship
___ 3. coddled		C. to boast or brag
___ 4. implacable		D. a group of twenty items
___ 5. score		E. a handle of a bladed instrument
___ 6. hafts		F. pulled or drawn tight
___ 7. hawser		G. incapable of appeasement

Odyssey-Vocabulary Worksheet Books XXIII - XXIV

Part I: Using Prior Knowledge and Contextual Clues
　　Below are the sentences in which the vocabulary words appear in the text. Read the sentence. Use any clues you can find in the sentence combined with your prior knowledge, and write what you think the underlined words mean in the space provided.

1-2. "Someone killed them,...a god, sick of their arrogance and brutal malice..."

3. "She turned then to descend, her heart in tumult."

4. "This is a shroud I weave for Laertes when death comes to him on his bier

5. "Break off this bitter skirmish; end your bloodshed

Part II: Determining the Meaning
　　Match the vocabulary words to their dictionary definitions

　　___ 1. arrogance　　　　A. disorderly commotion
　　___ 2. brutal　　　　　　B. insolent pride
　　___ 3. tumult　　　　　　C. a minor conflict or dispute
　　___ 4. bier　　　　　　　D. a stand on which a coffin or corpse is placed
　　___ 5. skirmish　　　　　E. cruel or harsh

ANSWER KEY - VOCABULARY
The Odyssey

Books I-II	Books III-IV	Books V-VI	Books VII-VIII
1. E	1. F	1. J	1. B
2. J	2. D	2. F	2. E
3. A	3. J	3. A	3. J
4. G	4. A	4. I	4. G
5. B	5. I	5. B	5. A
6. I	6. B	6. G	6. I
7. D	7. H	7. C	7. C
8. C	8. C	8. E	8. H
9. H	9. G	9. H	9. D
10. F	10. E	10. D	10. F

Book IX	Books X-XII	Books XIII-XIV	Books XV-XVI
1. H	1. B	1. D	1. G
2. C	2. I	2. G	2. C
3. G	3. A	3. A	3. J
4. D	4. C	4. B	4. E
5. B	5. G	5. F	5. I
6. I	6. D	6. E	6. B
7. F	7. H	7. C	7. H
8. E	8. F		8. A
9. A	9. E		9. F
			10. D

Books XVII-XVIII	Books XIX-XX	Books XXI-XXII	Books XXIII-XXIV
1. G	1. D	1. C	1. B
2. A	2. H	2. F	2. E
3. F	3. E	3. A	3. A
4. B	4. A	4. G	4. D
5. C	5. I	5. D	5. C
6. D	6. B	6. E	
7. E	7. F	7. B	
	8. C		
	9. G		

DAILY LESSONS

LESSONS ONE AND TWO

Objectives
1. To introduce the *Odyssey* unit
2. To give students some background information about Homer and *The Odyssey*
3. To associate prior knowledge with new information about *The Odyssey*
4. To preview the study questions and vocabulary for Books I-II
5. To read Books I-II

NOTE: This introductory lesson requires that you have acquired a film or filmstrip about Homer and *The Odyssey*. If you are not able to find a film, use the introductory materials found in "A Few Notes about Homer...." at the beginning of this unit plan.

Activity #1
Create a wordstorm! Write the word "odyssey" on the board and ask students to call out any related words that they think of. Record all of them on the board. Have one student copy the list so you can refer to it at a later date.

Activity #2
Distribute the materials students will use in this unit. Explain in detail how students are to use these materials.

<u>Study Guides</u> Students should read the study guide questions for each reading assignment prior to beginning the reading assignment to get a feeling for what events and ideas are important in the section they are about to read. After reading the section, students will (as a class or individually) answer the questions to review the important events and ideas from that section of the book. Students should keep the study guides as study materials for the unit test.

<u>Vocabulary</u> Prior to reading a reading assignment, students will do vocabulary work related to the section of the book they are about to read. Following the completion of the reading of the book, there will be a vocabulary review of all the words used in the vocabulary assignments. Students should keep their vocabulary work as study materials for the unit test.

<u>Reading Assignment Sheet</u> You need to fill in the reading assignment sheet to let students know by when their reading has to be completed. You can either write the assignment sheet up on a side blackboard or bulletin board and leave it there for students to see each day, or you can "ditto" copies for each student to have. In either case, you should advise students to become very familiar with the reading assignments so they know what is expected of them.

<u>Extra Activities Center</u> The resource pages of this unit contains suggestions for an extra library of related books and articles in your classroom as well as crossword and word search puzzles. Make an extra activities center in your room where you will keep these materials for students to use. (Bring the books and articles in from the library and keep several copies of

the puzzles on hand.) Explain to students that these materials are available for students to use when they finish reading assignments or other class work early.

    Nonfiction Assignment Sheet Explain to students that they each are to read at least one non-fiction piece from the in-class library at some time during the unit. Students will fill out a nonfiction assignment sheet after completing the reading to help you evaluate their reading experiences and to help the students think about and evaluate their own reading experiences. The nonfiction reading assignment in this unit is incorporated into the Group Theme Project.

    Books Each school has its own rules and regulations regarding student use of school books. Advise students of the procedures that are normal for your school. Preview the book. Look at the covers, frontmatter, and index. Glance at some of the drawings.

Activity #3
    Show students how to preview the study questions and discuss the directions for completing the vocabulary worksheets for Books I-II of *The Odyssey*. Give students about fifteen minutes to complete the vocabulary worksheet.

Activity #4
    Have students read Books I-II in class. If you have access to audio tapes of *The Odyssey*, have students follow along in their texts as you play the audio tapes.

NONFICTION ASSIGNMENT SHEET
(To be completed after reading the required nonfiction article)

Name _____ Date _____

Title of Nonfiction Read _____

Written By _____ Publication Date _____

I. Factual Summary: Write a short summary of the piece you read.

II. Vocabulary
    1. With which vocabulary words in the piece did you encounter some degree of difficulty?

    2. How did you resolve your lack of understanding with these words?

III. Interpretation: What was the main point the author wanted you to get from reading his work?

IV. Criticism
    1. With which points of the piece did you agree or find easy to accept? Why?

    2. With which points of the piece did you disagree or find difficult to believe? Why?

V. Personal Response: What do you think about this piece? OR How does this piece influence your ideas?

LESSON THREE

Objectives
1. To review the main events and ideas in Books I-II
2. To preview the study questions and vocabulary for Books III-IV
3. To read Books III-IV & V-VI
4. To give students practice reading orally
5. To evaluate students' oral reading

Activity #1
Give students a few minutes to formulate answers for the study guide questions for Books I-II, and then discuss the answers to the questions in detail. Write the answers on the board or overhead transparency so students can have the correct answers for study purposes. Note: It is a good practice in public speaking and leadership skills for individual students to take charge of leading the discussions of the study questions. Perhaps a different student could go to the front of the class and lead the discussion each day that the study questions are discussed during this unit. Of course, the teacher should guide the discussion when appropriate and be sure to fill in any gaps the students leave.

Activity #2
Give students about fifteen minutes to preview the study questions for Books III-IV of *The Odyssey* and to do the related vocabulary work.

Activity #2
Have students read Books III-IV of *The Odyssey* out loud in class. You probably know the best way to get readers with your class; pick students at random, ask for volunteers, or use whatever method works best for your group. If you have not yet completed an oral reading evaluation for your students this period, this would be a good opportunity to do so. A form is included with this unit for your convenience.

Activity #3
Tell students that prior to your next class meeting they should have completed the assignment for Activity #2 and should have previewed the study questions, have done the vocabulary work, and have read Books V-VI.

ORAL READING EVALUATION - *The Odyssey*

Name _____ Class____ Date _____

SKILL	EXCELLENT	GOOD	AVERAGE	FAIR	POOR
Fluency	5	4	3	2	1
Clarity	5	4	3	2	1
Audibility	5	4	3	2	1
Pronunciation	5	4	3	2	1
_____	5	4	3	2	1
_____	5	4	3	2	1

Total _____   Grade _____

Comments:

LESSON FOUR

Objectives
1. To review the main events and ideas from Books III-VI
2. To preview the study questions for Books VII-IX
3. To familiarize students with the vocabulary in Books VII-IX
4. To read books VII-IX

Activity #1
Give students a few minutes to formulate answers for the study guide questions for Books III-VI, and then discuss the answers to the questions in detail. Write the answers on the board or overhead transparency so students can have the correct answers for study purposes.

Activity #2
Give students about fifteen minutes to preview the study questions for Books VII-VIII of *The Odyssey* and to do the related vocabulary work.

Activity #3
Have students read Books VII-IX of *The Odyssey* in class. Try partner reading for a change of pace. One student reads aloud while the other follows along and listens. Partners switch roles as they desire.

Activity #4
Tell students that prior to your next class period they should have completed the prereading and reading work through Book IX of *The Odyssey*.

LESSON FIVE

Objectives
1. To check to see that students read Books VII-VIII
2. To review the main ideas and events from Books VII-VIII
3. To give students the opportunity to practice using the library/media center's resources
4. To give students time to get materials for their nonfiction reading assignment

Activity #1
Quiz - Distribute quizzes and give students about 10 minutes to complete them. (Note: The quizzes may either be the short answer study guides or the multiple choice version for Books VII-VIII.) Have students exchange papers. Grade the quizzes as a class. Collect the papers for recording the grades. (If you used the multiple choice version as a quiz, take a few minutes to discuss the answers for the short answer version if your students are using the short answer version for their study guides.)

Activity #2
Take students to the library/media center to find articles, books, etc. about nonfiction topics related to *The Odyssey*. Some suggested topics are: ships, sailing, travel, Greek cooking, famous Greeks, homelessness, Greek civilization past & present, mystical women (things like mermaids, etc.), the role of women in Greek society, Greek ceremonies through history, Greek and Roman gods, the Greek alphabet, Greek architecture, and athletics.

LESSON SIX

Objectives
1. To review the main ideas and events from Book IX
2. To do the prereading work for Books X-XIV
3. To read Books X-XIV

Activity #1
Give students a few minutes to formulate answers for the study guide questions for Book IX, and then discuss the answers to the questions in detail. Write the answers on the board or overhead transparency so students can have the correct answers for study purposes.

Activity #2
Give students about ten-fifteen minutes to do the prereading work for Books X-XII.

Activity #3
If you have audio tapes for *The Odyssey*, play the tape(s) for Books X-XII during your class time.

Activity #4
Tell students that prior to Lesson Eight (give students a day and a date) they should have completed the prereading work and the reading through Book XIV. If there is time left in this class period, students may begin to work on this assignment.

LESSON SEVEN

Objective
To stimulate students' independent thinking

Activity
Choose for your students or let your students choose one of the class or individual projects listed on the next page. Be sure to tell students when their projects will be due. You may wish to have students report back to the whole class after they have completed their projects. Give students this class period to begin working on their project(s).

GROUP OR INDIVIDUAL PROJECTS - *The Odyssey*

PROJECT ONE

In Books XVII-XXIII we see Odysseus as a beggar. He is very poorly treated by the suitors, who are from the upper class citizenry of Ithaka. In all ages, there have been poor and homeless people. Research the plight of the homeless in different countries, or in different centuries. Or, focus on what is being done in the United States currently to aid these unfortunate people. Another approach would be to research the way that different religions deal with the homeless problem. Reports should include, whenever possible, statistics and pictures. If possible, visit a homeless shelter and talk to the inhabitants. Organize a project to bring food or clothes to the shelter on a regular basis.

PROJECT TWO

Part of Odysseus' journey included visits to fantasy-type lands. Other authors have also used this theme. Research this theme, read some of the other works, and compare the journeys of the various heroes.

PROJECT THREE

Dramatize sections of *The Odyssey*. Choose a book or section of *The Odyssey* to dramatize. Rewrite the narrative as a script, design costumes, and make a production of the scene or book on videotape. Consider making your videotape available to local elementary or middle schools, convalescent centers, or others in the community for entertainment.

LESSON EIGHT

Objectives
    1. To review the main events of Books X-XIV
    2. To check to see that students did the reading assignment
    3. To assign the pre-reading, vocabulary and reading work for Books XV-XVI
    4. To give students time to work on their project(s)

Activity #1
    Give students a quiz on Books X-XIV. Use either the short answer or multiple choice form of the study guide questions as a quiz so that in discussing the answers to the quiz you also answer the study guide questions. Collect the papers for grade recording.

Activity #2
    Give students this class period to continue working on their project(s).

Activity #3
    Tell students that prior to their next class period, they must have completed the pre-reading, vocabulary and reading work for Books XV-XVI.

LESSON NINE

Objectives
    1. To review the main ideas and events of Books XV-XVI
    2. To preview the study questions for Books XVII-XX
    3. To do the vocabulary work for Books XVII-XX
    4. To read Books XVII-XX

Activity #1
    Discuss the answers to the study guide questions for Books XV-XVI. Write the answers on the board for students to copy down for study use later.

Activity #2
    Give students about fifteen minutes to preview the study questions and to do the vocabulary work for Book XVII.

Activity #3
    Have students read Book XVII in class. For a change of pace, have students try "Radio Reading." Students sit in groups of 4-6. One is the radio reader, and the others listen and/or follow along in their books. Each of the members of the group has the option of reading aloud. Tell students that prior to your next class period, they should have completed the prereading and reading work for Books XVIII-XX. If time remains in this class period, they may begin working on this assignment.

LESSON TEN

<u>Objectives</u>
    1. To give students the opportunity to practice writing their own opinions
    2. To get students to think about the characters and events in *The Odyssey*
    3. To give the teacher the opportunity to evaluate students' writing skills

<u>Activity</u>
    Distribute Writing Assignment #1. Discuss the directions in detail and give students ample time to complete the assignment.

LESSON ELEVEN

<u>Objectives</u>
    1. To review the main ideas and events from Books XVII-XX
    2. To preview the study questions and vocabulary for Books XXI-XXIV
    3. To read Books XXI-XXIV

<u>Activity #1</u>
    Discuss the answers to the study guide questions for Books XVII-XX. Write the answers on the board for students to copy down for study use later.

<u>Activity #2</u>
    Tell students that prior to your next class period, they should have completed the prereading and reading work for Books XXI-XXIV. Students may use the remainder of this class period to begin working on this assignment.

WRITING ASSIGNMENT #1 - *The Odyssey*

PROMPT

An opinion is a belief that you hold about a certain topic. Opinions cannot be proved and are therefore contrasted with facts, which can be proved. Adjectives are often used when giving opinions. ("That's a <u>beautiful</u> coat," or "what a <u>boring</u> lecture.")

No doubt you have opinions about many of the characters and events in *The Odyssey*. Choose four characters or events from the story and give your opinions about each.

PREWRITING

Think about the characters and events you have read about in *The Odyssey*. Refer to your study guides or the text to refresh your memory. Which ones do you have the strongest opinions about -- which did you like the best or least, think the most interesting or most ridiculous, etc.? Jot down the four characters and/or events about which you have definite opinions.

DRAFTING

Write your composition in the form of a chart. Briefly summarize the facts in a left-hand column, and then write your opinion in a right-hand column. Use complete sentences.

PROMPT

When you finish the rough draft of your paper, ask a student who sits near you to read it. After reading your rough draft, he/she should tell you what he/she liked best about your work, which parts were difficult to understand, and ways in which your work could be improved. Reread your paper considering your critic's comments, and make the corrections you think are necessary. Ask your classmate what he/she thought of each of the characters/events you chose for your assignment.

PROOFREADING

Do a final proofreading of your paper double-checking your grammar, spelling, organization, and the clarity of your ideas.

LESSON TWELVE

Objective
To review all of the vocabulary work done in this unit

Activity
Choose one (or more) of the vocabulary review activities listed below and spend your class period as directed in the activity. Some of the materials for these review activities are located in the Extra Activities section of this unit. Since there are over 100 words from all the books combined, we have chosen a list of about 50 words for which students will be responsible.

VOCABULARY REVIEW ACTIVITIES

1. Divide your class into two teams and have an old-fashioned spelling or definition bee.

2. Give each of your students (or students in groups of two, three or four) an *Odyssey* Vocabulary Word Search Puzzle. The person (group) to find all of the vocabulary words in the puzzle first wins.

3. Give students an *Odyssey* Vocabulary Word Search Puzzle without the word list. The person or group to find the most vocabulary words in the puzzle wins.

4. Use an *Odyssey* Vocabulary Crossword Puzzle. Put the puzzle onto a transparency on the overhead projector (so everyone can see it) and do the puzzle together as a class.

5. Give students an *Odyssey* Vocabulary Matching Worksheet to do.

6. Divide your class into two teams. Use the *Odyssey* vocabulary words with their letters jumbled as a word list. Student 1 from Team A faces off against Student 1 from Team B. You write the first jumbled word on the board. The first student (1A or 1B) to unscramble the word wins the chance for his/her team to score points. If 1A wins the jumble, go to student 2A and give him/her a definition. He/she must give you the correct spelling of the vocabulary word which fits that definition. If he/she does, Team A scores a point, and you give student 3A a definition for which you expect a correctly spelled matching vocabulary word. Continue giving Team A definitions until some team member makes an incorrect response. An incorrect response sends the game back to the jumbled-word face off, this time with students 2A and 2B. Instead of repeating giving definitions to the first few students of each team, continue with the student after the one who gave the last incorrect response on the team. For example, if Team B wins the jumbled-word face-off, and student 5B gave the last incorrect answer for Team B, you would start this round of definition questions with student 6B, and so on. The team with the most points wins!

7. Have students write a story in which they correctly use as many vocabulary words as possible. Have students read their compositions orally! Post the most original compositions on your bulletin board.

VOCABULARY LIST - *The Odyssey*
This is the list of words on which you will be tested.

PLUNDERED	Robbed of goods by force
VALOR	Courage; boldness
CLARION	Shrill and clear
AUDACITY	Boldness or daring
VIGILANCE	Watchfulness
PRECEDENCE	Priority; going in advance
INSIDIOUS	Working or spreading harmfully in a sly way
VIE	To compete or strive for victory
FEIGN	To pretend
PROMONTORY	A high ridge of land or rock jutting into the sea
PUNGENT	Having a sharp, bitter taste
LUMINOUS	Emitting self-generated light
PERPLEXITY	The state of being puzzled or confused
OBLIVION	The state of being completely forgotten
FLOUT	To show contempt or scorn
DEFERENCE	Courteous respect
AUSPICIOUS	Attended by favorable circumstances
COMELY	Attractive; handsome; graceful
CONTENTIOUSLY	In a quarrelsome way
GUILE	Treacherous cunning; craftiness
MUSTER	To assemble or gather
PROFUSION	Abundance; extravagance
PRODIGIOUS	Impressively great in size
APPALLED	Filled with dismay
STALWART	Having physical strength
SUPPLICATION	A humble or earnest plea
SUCCUMBED	Yielded or submitted to an overpowering force
CALAMITOUS	Causing or involving disaster
TIMOROUS	Full of apprehensiveness
MEAGER	Deficient in quality, fullness, or extent
DISSIMULATION	Concealing or disguising
CACHE	A hole or hiding place
DERELICT	A vagrant or social outcast
CHATTELS	Articles of personal, movable property
BENEVOLENT	Kind
CANDOR	Frankness; sincerity

Odyssey Vocabulary List Continued

RANCOR	Bitter, long-lasting resentment
STEEPED	Soaked
DOLE	To distribute in small portions
PATRIMONY	An inheritance from a father
MORTIFIED	Shamed or humiliated
REBUKE	Criticize or reprove sharply
WINDFALL	A sudden and unexpected piece of good fortune
RESPLENDENT	Brilliant
VIVACITY	Liveliness
AUGURY	Interpreting signs and omens
PITH	The essential or central part of anything
OBSTINACY	Stubbornness
CODDLED	Treated indulgently; babied
IMPLACABLE	Incapable of appeasement

LESSON THIRTEEN

Objectives
    1. To review the main ideas and events from Books XXI-XXIV
    2. To give students time to prepare for a discussion of *The Odyssey*

Activity #1
    Discuss the answers to the study guide questions for Books XXI-XXIV. Write the answers on the board for students to copy down for study use later.

Activity #2
    Choose the questions from the Extra Discussion Questions/Writing Assignments which seem most appropriate for your students. A class discussion of these questions is most effective if students have been given the opportunity to formulate answers to the questions prior to the discussion. To this end, you may either have all the students formulate answers to all the questions, divide your class into groups and assign one or more questions to each group, or you could assign one question to each student in your class. The option you choose will make a difference in the amount of class time needed for this activity. The class discussion of these questions is scheduled for Lesson Fifteen.

NOTE: The use of graphic organizers may be helpful to students in preparing their answers. Encourage them to use any diagrams or graphics that they feel are necessary.

LESSON FOURTEEN

Objectives
    1. To give students the opportunity to practice writing to persuade
    2. To give the teacher the opportunity to evaluate students' writing skills
    3. To review characters and character motivations in *The Odyssey*

Activity
    Distribute Writing Assignment #2. Discuss the directions in detail and give students ample time to complete the assignment.

EXTRA WRITING ASSIGNMENTS/DISCUSSION QUESTIONS - *The Odyssey*

Interpretation

1. Identify and explain the qualities which were considered of greatest value for a man to possess at this period in time.

2. In what times (tenses) are the various books of the narrative told? Why?

3. What are the main conflicts in the story? Are all the conflicts resolved? Explain how those that are resolved are resolved, and explain why those that are not resolved are not.

4. Explain the importance and influence of the setting(s) in the story.

5. Which characters are "good guys" and which characters are "bad guys"? Explain your choices.

Critical

6. Discuss the virtue of hospitality in *The Odyssey* (both those who honor it and those who abuse it).

7. Are Odysseus' actions believably motivated? Explain why or why not.

8. Does Odysseus develop or change as a result of his adventures? Explain how he does if he does, or why he does not if he does not.

9. Argue for or against the destruction of the suitors.

10. Describe the role of (human) women in *The Odyssey*.

11. Compare the homecomings of Odysseus and Agamemnon.

12. Describe Telemakhos' maturation as he develops in the story.

13. Compare and contrast *The Odyssey* with a modern American novel.

14. Compare and contrast Penelope and Klytaimnestra.

15. How does *The Odyssey* reflect the times in which it was written?

16. Where would you locate the climax of the narrative? Why?

17. Explain the structure of the narrative. Use graphic organizers, such as a time line or a book map, if desired.

The Odyssey Extra Discussion Questions page 2

18. What is an epic, and how does *The Odyssey* fit that definition?

19. Explain the role of revenge in the story.

20. Which characters in the story parallel each other?

21. Homer's narrative does not start at the beginning of Odysseus' journey but rather close to the end of it. Why do you think Homer chose this place (Odysseus on Kalypso's Island) to begin the epic?

22. Compare and contrast the significance of the adventures that Odysseus had in the nine years prior to his stay with Kalypso with the adventures he had after leaving the island. Which are more important?

23. Compare and contrast the pictures of Odysseus from the beginning and the end of the novel.

Critical/Personal Response

24. Is the story of *The Odyssey* believable? Explain why or why not.

25. Do you think the repetition of so many of the lines in the narrative enhances or detracts from it? Why?

26. Pick a major character and explain why you like or dislike him/her.

27. Identify the speaker and explain whether or not you agree with him: "I would rather follow the plow as thrall to another man, one with no land allotted him and not much to live on, than be king over all the perished dead."

28. Considering all the advice and help that Odysseus receives from the gods, do you think he is a brave man or merely a lucky man?

29. Why do you suppose being skilled at athletic games was so important to Odysseus and his contemporaries?

30. Homer's time scheme is quite complicated. Argue for or against his use of this time scheme.

31. Did you enjoy reading *The Odyssey*? Why or why not?

32. If Odysseus were living today, where would he live and what would he be doing?

WRITING ASSIGNMENT #2 - *The Odyssey*

PROMPT

A persuasive letter or essay is written to change another's opinion of a situation or to get action taken in a matter. The issue should be one of personal importance to you but should involve more than personal taste. (For example, you should not try to persuade the school cafeteria to serve only pepperoni pizza because it is your favorite meal.) You should be able to gather evidence to support your ideas. In preparing to write a persuasive piece, you may first want to read the editorial pages from several newspapers. You may also want to talk to an attorney or sit in on a court case and listen to some of the persuasive arguments that are used.

Your assignment is to write one of the following persuasive arguments related to the *Odyssey* (or you may think of your own that is related to the book):
1. Write from the point of view of Telemakhos. Tell the suitors why they should leave.
2. Write from the point of view of one of the suitors. Tell why you should stay and why Penelope should choose you for her husband.
3. Help Athena argue with Zeus and Poseidon in favor of helping Odysseus return home.
4. Should Odysseus kill the suitors? Write from either side or as an observer.

PREWRITING

A persuasive paper will have a thesis statement. This tells your opinion and what you want the other reader to think or do. Write down a thesis statement for your composition. Words and phrases like "must," "should," "ought," "it is imperative that," and "it is essential that" add force and urgency to your thesis.

The next step in writing a persuasive paper is to gather evidence. Since you will be writing about events in a novel, the novel and critiques of it would be your best sources. Make sure to gather facts that support your opinion. Be aware of the opposing arguments so that you can defend your position against them. Keep your audience in mind. What do you know about them? What type of argument might be effective in changing their opinions? Write down several good arguments (reasons) you could use in your composition. Next to each, jot down some examples or facts from the story that will support those arguments.

Organize your arguments. You may want to write each argument on a separate index card and rank them numerically, one being the most important. Then decide on your order of presentation. You can arrange your arguments from most important to least, or vice versa. Make sure to use transition words (then, also, more important, in addition to, etc.) to link your ideas together. Recommend action. Be specific, yet brief.

DRAFTING

Write a paragraph of introduction in which you introduce your thesis statement. Write one good paragraph for each of your arguments, using a topic sentence and filling out the paragraph with examples and facts to support your statement. Write a concluding paragraph in which you recommend an action, summarize your arguments and bring your composition to a close.

Writing Assignment #2 *The Odyssey* Continued

PROMPT

When you finish the rough draft of your paper, ask a student who sits near you to read it. After reading your rough draft, he/she should tell you what he/she liked best about your work, which parts were difficult to understand, and ways in which your work could be improved. Reread your paper considering your critic's comments, and make the corrections you think are necessary.

PROOFREADING

Do a final proofreading of your paper double-checking your grammar, spelling, organization, and the clarity of your ideas.

LESSON FIFTEEN

Objective
  To discuss *The Odyssey* on interpretive and critical levels

Activity
  Students have had ample time to formulate answers to the questions in Lesson Fourteen and at home since then. Use this class time for your class discussion of the questions and the ideas presented by the questions. Be sure students take notes during the discussion so they have information to study for the unit test.

LESSON SIXTEEN

Objectives
  1. To widen the breadth of students' knowledge about the topics discussed or touched upon in *The Odyssey*
  2. To check students' nonfiction reading assignments

Activity
  Ask each student to give a brief oral report about the nonfiction articles he/she read for the unit project assignment. Your criteria for evaluating this report will vary depending on the level of your students. You may wish for students to give a complete report without using notes of any kind, or you may want students to read directly from a written report, or you may want to do something in between these two extremes. Just make students aware of your criteria in ample time for them to prepare their reports.

  Start with one student's report. After that, ask if anyone else in the class has read on a topic related to the first student's report. If no one has, choose another student at random. After each report, be sure to ask if anyone has a report related to the one just completed. That will help keep a continuity during the discussion of the reports. After all reports on a topic are given, take a minute to hold a short class discussion about the information students have just heard.

LESSONS SEVENTEEN AND EIGHTEEN

Objectives
1. To examine the character of Odysseus
2. To review the main events of *The Odyssey*
3. To have students practice their small group interaction skills

Activity #1

Divide your class into six groups--one group for each of the following characteristics:
1. Cunning and Quick Thinking
2. Bravery
3. Loyalty
4. Pride
5. Kindness
6. Generosity

Allow the groups time to find specific examples of their characteristics in the text. Each group member should be assigned specific books of the text to examine so that the work gets done quickly and so that each person has a specific task to do. Allow time for the group members to discuss and compile their findings. Each group should appoint a spokesperson to report the group's thoughts.

Activity #2

Ask each group's spokesperson to give the group's findings. Jot these down on the board or overhead projector in a chart and use the facts as a springboard for a discussion about each characteristic.

LESSON NINETEEN

Objectives
1. To give students the opportunity to practice writing to inform
2. To give the teacher the opportunity to evaluate students' writing skills
3. To review the main events of the book

Activity

Distribute Writing Assignment #3. Discuss the directions in detail and give students ample time to complete the assignment. While students are writing, call individual students to your desk or some other private area for a writing conference based on the first two writing assignments in this unit. An evaluation form is included in this unit for your convenience.

LESSON TWENTY

Activity

Choose one of the review games/activities suggested in this unit and spend your class time as directed there.

WRITING ASSIGNMENT #3 - *The Odyssey*

PROMPT

One way to write to inform is to write a newspaper article. News articles are written about important or unusual events. Odysseus had many adventures, any one of which would make an interesting news article.

Your assignment is to choose one event from *The Odyssey* and write it as a news article.

PREWRITING

Begin by making a list of some of the events in the story that most interested you. Then choose one to focus on. Pretend you are a reporter on the scene. Take notes about the event, remembering to answer the basic news questions: who, what, when, where, why and how. Add any additional details that you think might be interesting to your readers. Create a headline. The headline should be catchy and mention the main idea. It should also be brief. Try using alliteration, simile or metaphor, or a pun in the headline.

DRAFTING

When you write, keep your audience in mind. Are you writing for your peers, older people, or young children? You will want to customize your article by the use of appropriate vocabulary and sentence length.

A news story usually starts with a paragraph in which all the basic news questions are answered. That is followed by paragraphs which give the details of the story.

Your writing should be clear and concise so your readers will understand. Write in a lively, interesting way.

PROMPT

When you finish the rough draft of your paper, ask a student who sits near you to read it. After reading your rough draft, he/she should tell you what he/she liked best about your work, which parts were difficult to understand, and ways in which your work could be improved. Reread your paper considering your critic's comments, and make the corrections you think are necessary.

PROOFREADING

Do a final proofreading of your paper double-checking your grammar, spelling, organization, and the clarity of your ideas.

WRITING EVALUATION FORM - *The Odyssey*

Name _____ Date _____ Grade _____

Circle One For Each Item:

Grammar:	correct	errors noted on paper
Spelling:	correct	errors noted on paper
Punctuation:	correct	errors noted on paper
Legibility:	excellent	good fair poor
_____	excellent	good fair poor
_____	excellent	good fair poor

Strengths:

Weaknesses:

Comments/Suggestions:

REVIEW GAMES/ACTIVITIES - *The Odyssey*

1. Ask the class to make up a unit test for *The Odyssey*. The test should have 4 sections: matching, true/false, short answer, and essay. Students may use 1/2 period to make the test and then swap papers and use the other 1/2 class period to take a test a classmate has devised (open book). You may want to use the unit test included in this packet or take questions from the students' unit tests to formulate your own test.

2. Take 1/2 period for students to make up true and false questions (including the answers). Collect the papers and divide the class into two teams. Draw a big tic-tac-toe board on the chalk board. Make one team X and one team O. Ask questions to each side, giving each student one turn. If the question is answered correctly, that student's team's letter (X or O) is placed in the box. If the answer is incorrect, no letter is placed in the box. The object is to get three in a row like tic-tac-toe. You may want to keep track of the number of games won for each team.

3. Take 1/2 period for students to make up questions (true/false and short answer). Collect the questions. Divide the class into two teams. You'll alternate asking questions of individual members of teams A & B (like in a spelling bee). The question keeps going from A to B until it is correctly answered, then a new question is asked. A correct answer does not allow the team to get another question. Correct answers are +2 points; incorrect answers are -1 point.

4. Have students pair up and quiz each other from their study guides and class notes.

5. Give students an *Odyssey* crossword puzzle to complete.

6. Divide your class into two teams. Use the *Odyssey* crossword words with their letters jumbled as a word list. Student 1 from Team A faces off against Student 1 from Team B. You write the first jumbled word on the board. The first student (1A or 1B) to unscramble the word wins the chance for his/her team to score points. If 1A wins the jumble, go to student 2A and give him/her a clue. He/she must give you the correct word which matches that clue. If he/she does, Team A scores a point, and you give student 3A a clue for which you expect another correct response. Continue giving Team A clues until some team member makes an incorrect response. An incorrect response sends the game back to the jumbled-word face off, this time with students 2A and 2B. Instead of repeating giving clues to the first few students of each team, continue with the student after the one who gave the last incorrect response on the team. For example, if Team B wins the jumbled-word face-off, and student 5B gave the last incorrect answer for Team B, you would start this round of clue questions with student 6B, and so on. The team with the most points wins!

Review Games Page 2

8. Play What's My Line?. This is similar to the old television show. Students assume the roles of different characters from the epic. One student gives clues to the class or to a panel of contestants. The contestants try to guess the identity of the guest. Students may enjoy assisting you in creating rules and procedures for the game.

9. Play Jeopardy. Divide the class into two groups. Assign each group a category or book from the epic and have them devise answers for that category. Play the game according to the television show procedures.

10. Play Drawing in the Details. This is similar to Pictionary. Divide students into teams. A student from one team draws a scene from the epic. (You may want to specify the Book or section.) Drawings should be kept simple, to keep the pace lively. Students in the opposing team locate the scene in their books and read it aloud. If they are incorrect, the illustrator's team has a chance to guess. Involve students in setting up a scoring system and any other necessary rules.

UNIT TESTS

SHORT ANSWER UNIT TEST 1 - *The Odyssey*

I. Matching/Identify

____ 1. AGAMEMNON   A. God of the sun; owner of the cattle which Odysseus' men ate

____ 2. HELEN   B. Faithful wife to Odysseus

____ 3. HADES   C. Means by which Odysseus is recognized by his nurse

____ 4. HELIOS   D. Guarded by Hades; the place where the dead go

____ 5. ALKINOOS   E. Wife and murderer of Agamemnon

____ 6. SUITORS   F. The Kyclopes who captured Odysseus and his men & was blinded by them

____ 7. ZEUS   G. King of the gods; lives on Mt. Olympos

____ 8. POLYPHEMOS   H. King of Mycene; leader of Greeks during Trojan War; murdered by his wife & her lover

____ 9. UNDERWORLD   I. A mortal to whom the gods have given control of the winds

____ 10. MENELAUS   J. One of Odysseus' crew; was drunk & fell from Kirke's roof

____ 11. DISCUS   K. Father of Odysseus

____ 12. SCAR   L. Wife of Menelaus; the prince of Troy abducted her

____ 13. KLYTIAMNESTRA   M. God of the sea; seeks revenge on Odysseus for blinding his son

____ 14. GIFTS   N. King of the Phaiakians; gives Odysseus passage to Ithaka

____ 15. AEOLUS   O. Ruler of the underworld; brother to Zeus and Poseidon

____ 16. POSEIDON   P. A plate-like object that is thrown in contests

____ 17. OMEN   Q. The men who wanted to marry Penelope

____ 18. LAERTES   R. They were very important to the Greeks; presents

____ 19. PENELOPE   S. Sign of good or bad luck to come

____ 20. ELPENOR   T. Helen's husband; King of Sparta

Odyssey Short Answer Unit Test 1 Page 2

II. Short Answer

1. Why has Odysseus not yet returned from the Trojan War? (Book I)

2. Who are the men gathered at the home of Odysseus, and what do they want? (Book I)

3. What plan does Telemakhos enact in Books II and III?

4. Describe the homecoming of Agamemnon. (Book III)

5. Where has Odysseus been in the ten years since the end of the Trojan War?

Odyssey Short Answer Unit Test 1 Page 3

6. How does Odysseus finally resume his homeward journey?

7. Where does Odysseus go after he leaves Kalypso?

8. How does Penelope keep the suitors at bay?

9. How does Odysseus take revenge on the suitors?

10. How does Penelope test Odysseus? (Book XXIII)

11. How does the epic end? (Book XIV)

III. Essay
    Define the characteristics of an epic and explain how *The Odyssey* exemplifies them. You may include graphic organizers along with your essay.

Odyssey Short Answer Unit Test 1 Page 5

IV. Vocabulary

    Write down the vocabulary words. Go back later and write down the correct definition for each word.

1.

2.

3.

4.

5.

6.

7.

8.

9.

10.

SHORT ANSWER UNIT TEST 2 - *The Odyssey*

I. Matching/Identify

____ 1. AGAMEMNON   A. One of Odysseus' crew; was drunk & fell from Kirke's roof

____ 2. HELEN   B. Father of Odysseus

____ 3. HADES   C. Wife of Menelaus; the prince of Troy abducted her

____ 4. HELIOS   D. Faithful wife to Odysseus

____ 5. ALKINOOS   E. God of the sea; seeks revenge on Odysseus for blinding his son

____ 6. SUITORS   F. King of the Phaiakians; gives Odysseus passage to Ithaka

____ 7. ZEUS   G. Ruler of the underworld; brother to Zeus and Poseidon

____ 8. POLYPHEMOS   H. The men who wanted to marry Penelope

____ 9. UNDERWORLD   I. A mortal to whom the gods have given control of the winds

____ 10. MENELAUS   J. Helen's husband; King of Sparta

____ 11. DISCUS   K. Guarded by Hades; the place where the dead go

____ 12. SCAR   L. Sign of good or bad luck to come

____ 13. KLYTIAMNESTRA   M. Wife and murderer of Agamemnon

____ 14. GIFTS   N. The Kyclopes who captured Odysseus and his men & was blinded by them

____ 15. AEOLUS   O. King of the gods; lives on Mt. Olympos

____ 16. POSEIDON   P. They were very important to the Greeks; presents

____ 17. OMEN   Q. King of Mycene; leader of Greeks during Trojan War; murdered by his wife & her lover

____ 18. LAERTES   R. A plate-like object that is thrown in contests

____ 19. PENELOPE   S. Means by which Odysseus is recognized by his nurse

____ 20. ELPENOR   T. God of the sun; owner of the cattle which Odysseus' men ate

Odyssey Short Answer Unit Test 2 Page 2

II. Short Answer

1. Why is Menelaus to go to the Elysian Field instead of dying as other mortals do?

2. Odysseus is insulted by Seareach. What does he accuse Odysseus of being? Why?

3. Why do you think Homer interrupts the narrative to have Demodokos sing about the love of Ares and Aphrodite?

4. Why is it necessary for Odysseus to take some of his men by force away from the land of the Lotos-Eaters?

5. Why does Odysseus lead his men into Polyphemos' cave?

6. Why does Odysseus reveal his name to Polyphemos after he has escaped?

Odyssey Short Answer Unit Test 2 Page 3

7. Odysseus and his men come within sight of Ithaka. Why do they not land?

8. What does Teiresias tell Odysseus?

9. How doe the Seirines destroy men, and how do Odysseus and his men avoid destruction?

10. How does Poseidon react when he discovers that the Phaiakians have aided Odysseus in reaching Ithaka?

11. What instructions does Odysseus give to Telemakhos?

Odyssey Short Answer Unit Test 2 Page 4

12. What does Penelope do that makes Odysseus happy?

13. What contest does Penelope devise to test the suitors?

14. What is Odysseus' plan for killing the suitors?

15. What does Athena do when the families of the dead suitors attack Odysseus?

Odyssey Short Answer Unit Test 2 Page 4

III. Composition

    Identify and explain the qualities that were considered of greatest value for a man to have at the time of Odysseus and give specific examples of characters who had those qualities in *The Odyssey*.

IV. Vocabulary

    Write down the vocabulary words. Go back later and write down the correct definitions for the words.

1.

2.

3.

4.

5.

6.

7.

8.

9.

10.

ANSWER KEY: SHORT ANSWER UNIT TESTS - *The Odyssey*

The short answer questions are taken directly from the study guides.
If you need to look up the answers, you will find them in the study guide section.

Answers to the composition questions will vary depending on your
class discussions and the level of your students.

For the vocabulary section of the test, choose ten of the
words from the vocabulary lists to read orally for your students.

The answers to the matching section of the test are below.

Answers to the matching section of the Advanced Short Answer Unit Test
are the same as for Short Answer Unit Test #1.

Test #1	Test #2
1. H	1. Q
2. L	2. C
3. O	3. G
4. A	4. T
5. N	5. F
6. Q	6. H
7. G	7. O
8. F	8. N
9. D	9. K
10. T	10. J
11. P	11. R
12. C	12. S
13. E	13. M
14. R	14. P
15. I	15. I
16. M	16. E
17. S	17. L
18. K	18. B
19. B	19. D
20. J	20. A

MULTIPLE CHOICE UNIT TEST 1 - *The Odyssey*

I. Matching

____ 1. AGAMEMNON   A. Faithful wife to Odysseus

____ 2. HELEN   B. Means by which Odysseus is recognized by his nurse

____ 3. HADES   C. God of the sun; owner of the cattle which Odysseus's men ate

____ 4. HELIOS   D. Helen's husband; king of Sparta

____ 5. ALKINOOS   E. Sign of good or bad luck to come

____ 6. SUITORS   F. They were very important to the Greeks; presents

____ 7. ZEUS   G. King of the gods; lives on Mt. Olympos

____ 8. POLYPHEMOS   H. King of Mycene; leader of Greeks during Trojan War; murdered by his wife & her lover

____ 9. UNDERWORLD   I. A mortal to whom the gods have given control of the winds

____ 10. MENELAUS   J. One of Odysseus' crew; was drunk & fell from Kirke's roof

____ 11. DISCUS   K. Wife of Menelaus; the Prince of Troy abducted her

____ 12. SCAR   L. Father of Odysseus

____ 13. KLYTIAMNESTRA   M. God of the sea; seeks revenge on Odysseus for blinding his son

____ 14. GIFTS   N. King of the Phaiakians; gives Odysseus passage to Ithaka

____ 15. AEOLUS   O. A plate-like object that is thrown in contests

____ 16. POSEIDON   P. Ruler of the underworld; brother to Zeus and Poseidon

____ 17. OMEN   Q. The men who wanted to marry Penelope

____ 18. LAERTES   R. The Kyclopes who captured Odysseus & was blinded by them

____ 19. PENELOPE   S. Wife and murderer of Agamemnon

____ 20. ELPENOR   T. Guarded by Hades; the place where the dead go

Odyssey Multiple Choice Unit Test 1 Page 2

II. Multiple Choice

1. Why had Odysseus not yet returned home from the Trojan War?
    A. His boat had been damaged and he put into a port to have it fixed. The parts he needed were not available so he had to set his men to making them. The process was taking a long time.
    B. He had angered the god Poseidon by blinding Poseidon's son, Polyphemos. Poseidon has placed obstacles in his way, and Odysseus has not yet been able to return home.
    C. He stayed in Troy to help repair the damage done by the war. He felt it was the honorable thing to do.
    D. Odysseus was a man of adventure. He didn't really want to return home to his quiet, dull life, so he set out to have adventures instead.

2. At Odysseus' house in Ithaka, we are introduced to the suitors. What are they doing in the house?
    A. They are looking for eligible partners among Penelope's servant girls.
    B. They are offering their condolences to Penelope on the supposed death of Odysseus.
    C. They are looking to buy Penelope's fine furniture and household items should she decide to leave the house and move elsewhere.
    D. They are waiting for Penelope to make up her mind which one of them she will marry. While waiting, they are eating and drinking all of the food in the house.

3. To whom does Athena refer when she says: "They all would find death was quick, and marriage a painful matter?"
    A. She refers to the young virgins in Ithaka.
    B. She refers to the Trojans.
    C. She refers to the suitors.
    D. She refers to the widows left after the war.

4. What happens at the homecoming of Agamemnon?
    A. He is honored by the people and sees his new son for the first time.
    B. His family has kept the homecoming a secret so they can greet him privately. He is pleased.
    C. He is murdered by his wife, Klytaimnestra, and her lover, Aigisthos.
    D. Athena appears and praises him for his bravery.

5. Why is Menelaus to go to the Elysian Field instead of dying as other mortals do?
    A. His offerings to the gods are so far superior to all of the others that they awarded him that privilege.
    B. It was a promise that Athena made long ago to his mother.
    C. He is be an inspiration to other mortals, that a valiant and honest life has rewards.
    D. He is the husband of Helen, and son-in-law of Zeus, and he will not die.

Odyssey Multiple Choice Unit Test 1 Page 3

6. Which god or goddess brings a message from Zeus to Kalypso?
    A. Kadmos, the ship builder's daughter, does.
    B. Hermes does.
    C. Leukothea, a sea nymph, finds him.
    D. Amphitrite, the chief maid, does.

7. What happens to Odysseus on the eighteenth day, just as he sights the shores of Skheria?
    A. He is attacked by a great whale who swallows the raft. Odysseus manages to swim to safety.
    B. Poseidon, returning from a vacation in Ethiopia, sees the raft. In a rage he creates a storm which destroys the raft.
    C. He gets a severe sunburn and falls into a feverish coma. When he awakens he doesn't know where he is.
    D. He sees a mirage of a bucket of cool water, created by one of the gods. He is thirsty and drinks most of it, then gets violently ill.

8. What help does Ino give to Odysseus?
    A. She creates a magic ship for him.
    B. She sends a pod of dolphins to surround and protect his ship.
    C. She give him her magic veil which allows him to survive the long swim to Skheria.
    D. She calms the wind so the waves are not too big.

9. Odysseus is insulted by Seareach. What does he accuse Odysseus of being?
    A. Seareach accuses Odysseus of being a spy who wants to steal the secrets of the Phaikians' seafaring skills.
    B. He accuses Odysseus of being a fortune-hunter who only wants to marry a rich wife and live comfortably on her wealth.
    C. Seareach accuses Odysseus of being a man concerned only with business and profits and not with being an athlete.
    D. He accuses Odysseus of being a curse sent from the gods to destroy their way of life.

10. Why is it necessary for Odysseus to take some of his men by force away from the land of the Lotos-Eaters?
    A. The lotos fruit contained a magical drug that made them want to stay and eat more.
    B. The lotos fruit gave them panic attacks. They became fearful of embarking on another sea voyage.
    C. The lotos fruit paralyzed them and they were not able to leave by themselves.
    D. The lotos fruit made them fall in love with the women of the land and not want to leave.

Odyssey Multiple Choice Unit Test 1 Page 4

11. How is Odysseus able to wound Polyphemos?
    A. Odysseus poisons the wine and makes Polyphemos so sick that he is unable to defend himself.
    B. Odysseus and his men use a log sharpened on one end and drive it into his eye while he sleeps.
    C. Odysseus drives his sword through Polyphemos' liver.
    D. Odysseus and his men set Polyphemos on fire while he is milking the goats.

12. Odysseus and his men come within sight of Ithaka. Why do they not land?
    A. They are afraid they will not be remembered and will be killed as intruders.
    B. They want to wait until they have time to clean up and properly prepare themselves.
    C. The men think the bag from Aeolus contains treasure that Odysseus is keeping for himself. While Odysseus is sleeping, they open the bag. The winds escape and they are blown back to the Aeolan island.
    D. The ship is sunk on a reef.

13. Why must Odysseus visit the house of Hades?
    A. He has to get magical supplies for his ship, and Hades is the only place to get them.
    B. He must consult with the blind prophet Teiresias, who will tell Odysseus all he needs to know about getting home.
    C. He must atone for his past misbehavior before he can go home.
    D. He has to deliver the dead crewmen.

14. What does Odysseus promise Elpenor?
    A. He promises to return to Kirke's island and bury Elpenor's body.
    B. He promises to tell of Elpenor's brave deeds wherever he tells the story of his own adventures.
    C. He promises to take care of Elpenor's wife and children.
    D. He promises to avenge Elpenor's death.

15. How do Odysseus and his men avoid destruction by the Seirines?
    A. Odysseus orders his men to plug their ears with beeswax and has them lash him to the mast.
    B. They sing their own songs in the loudest possible voices, to drown out the sound of the Seirines.
    C. Athena puts all of the men into a magical sleep and guides the boat through herself.
    D. They throw trinkets and pieces of brightly colored cloth onto the island. The Seirines are fascinated with these items and forget to sing.

Odyssey Multiple Choice Unit Test 1 Page 5

16. Telemakhos receives an omen as he is about to depart. What is it, and what does it mean?
    A. Three dark clouds travel across the sun. Those who see it think it means that something terrible will happen in three days.
    B. He sees a double rainbow over the bow of the ship. He thinks it is a good luck sign, that he will have a safe journey.
    C. A mountain eagle holding a white goose in its talons flies to the right over the horses. Helen interprets the sign to mean that Odysseus will soon return to Ithaka and take revenge on the suitors.
    D. A pod of dolphins surround the ship. The crew thinks this means that they are at last in Poseidon's good graces.

17. Odysseus has a plan that he shares with Eumaios. What is it?
    A. Odysseus will dress in his finest clothing and boldly enter his house.
    B. He will disguise himself as a suitor and try to win Penelope himself.
    C. Odysseus plans to go to his own house and ask for a job as a servant for the suitors.
    D. He will go to town and talk to the families of the suitors, and ask them to remove the suitors from his house.

18. What instructions does Odysseus give to Telemakhos?
    A. He tells him to take Penelope away into a special hiding place in the woods and wait for a signal when it will be safe to come back. He says not to tell anyone else of the hiding place and to make sure they are not followed.
    B. He tells him to go home and act like a madman and threaten the suitors. Then he should lock himself and Penelope in her quarters and send his servant to Odysseus when this has been accomplished.
    C. He tells him to go home and wait for his father's arrival as a beggar. He warns Telemakhos not to interfere if the suitors are rude but to wait for the signal to hide all weapons except their own. He also reminds Telemakhos not to let anyone know that he (Odysseus) has returned.
    D. He tells Telemakhos to go to the house disguised as another suitor. He should try to get the others into jealous quarrels and keep them distracted.

19. What occurs between Odysseus and Iros? Why?
    A. They have a debate on who the most promising suitor is.
    B. They have a fist fight to decide which beggar may stay and which may leave.
    C. Iros thinks he recognizes the beggar as Odysseus. Odysseus has to deny it and distract Iros by talking about food and women.
    D. They plot together to rob Penelope's house and blame it on the suitors.

Odyssey Multiple Choice Unit Test 1 Page 6

20. What does Penelope do that makes Odysseus happy?
    A. She refuses to see the suitors and banishes all of them to the courtyard.
    B. She tells the suitors she will never marry again, even if Odysseus is dead.
    C. She offers sacrifice to the gods and prays for her husband's safe return.
    D. She enriches the house by requesting expensive gifts from the suitors.

21. What contest does Penelope devise to test the suitors?
    A. She says she will marry the man who wins against all of the others in a sword fight to the death.
    B. She decides whoever can string the great bow of Odysseus and send an arrow through the iron of twelve axes shall be her husband.
    C. She tells them that whoever is able to move her husband's bed shall be her husband.
    D. She says she will marry the man who will give her her weight in gold.

22. How does Penelope test Odysseus?
    A. She asks for details of their wedding and the birth of Telemakhos.
    B. She tells the servants to bring out his bed and then waits for his reaction.
    C. She asks him to name all of her relatives.
    D. She has Eurycleia identify him and then inspects the scar on his leg herself.

23. What does Athena do when the families of the dead suitors attack Odysseus?
    A. She kills all of the male relatives of the suitors.
    B. She makes Odysseus give gifts to the families of the suitors.
    C. She makes both sides pledge peace.
    D. She puts a protective mist around Odysseus so his enemies can't hurt him.

Odyssey Multiple Choice Unit Test 1 Page 7

III. Composition

1. Compare the homecomings of Odysseus and Agamemnon.

2. Compare and contrast Penelope and Klytiamnestra.

3. Discuss the virtue of hospitality in *The Odyssey* (both those who honor it and those who abuse it.)

Odyssey Multiple Choice Unit Test 1 Page 7

IV. Vocabulary - Match the correct definitions to the words.

____ 1. SUPPLICATION   A. Yielded or submitted to an overpowering force

____ 2. PRECEDENCE   B. Incapable of appeasement

____ 3. REBUKE   C. Robbed of goods by force

____ 4. SUCCUMBED   D. Frankness; sincerity

____ 5. TIMOROUS   E. To distribute in small portions

____ 6. IMPLACABLE   F. Soaked

____ 7. COMELY   G. The state of being puzzled or confused

____ 8. DOLE   H. Concealing or disguising

____ 9. CANDOR   I. Impressively great in size

____ 10. PRODIGIOUS   J. Criticize or reprove sharply

____ 11. CLARION   K. Emitting self-generated light

____ 12. DISSIMULATION   L. Filled with dismay

____ 13. PERPLEXITY   M. To pretend

____ 14. PLUNDERED   N. A humble or earnest plea

____ 15. FEIGN   O. Shrill and clear

____ 16. VIGILANCE   P. Attractive; handsome; graceful

____ 17. PROMONTORY   Q. Full of apprehensiveness

____ 18. STEEPED   R. Priority; going in advance

____ 19. APPALLED   S. Watchfulness

____ 20. LUMINOUS   T. A high ridge of land or rock jutting into the sea

MULTIPLE CHOICE UNIT TEST 2 - *The Odyssey*

I. Matching

_____ 1. AGAMEMNON — A. One of Odysseus' crew; was drunk & fell from Kirke's roof

_____ 2. HELEN — B. Father of Odysseus

_____ 3. HADES — C. Wife of Menelaus; the prince of Troy abducted her

_____ 4. HELIOS — D. Faithful wife to Odysseus

_____ 5. ALKINOOS — E. God of the sea; seeks revenge on Odysseus for blinding his son

_____ 6. SUITORS — F. King of the Phaiakians; gives Odysseus passage to Ithaka

_____ 7. ZEUS — G. Ruler of the underworld; brother to Zeus and Poseidon

_____ 8. POLYPHEMOS — H. The men who wanted to marry Penelope

_____ 9. UNDERWORLD — I. A mortal to whom the gods have given control of the winds

_____ 10. MENELAUS — J. Helen's husband; King of Sparta

_____ 11. DISCUS — K. Guarded by Hades; the place where the dead go

_____ 12. SCAR — L. Sign of good or bad luck to come

_____ 13. KLYTIAMNESTRA — M. Wife and murderer of Agamemnon

_____ 14. GIFTS — N. The Kyclopes who captured Odysseus and his men & was blinded by them

_____ 15. AEOLUS — O. King of the gods; lives on Mt. Olympos

_____ 16. POSEIDON — P. They were very important to the Greeks; presents

_____ 17. OMEN — Q. King of Mycene; leader of Greeks during Trojan War; murdered by his wife & her lover

_____ 18. LAERTES — R. A plate-like object that is thrown in contests

_____ 19. PENELOPE — S. Means by which Odysseus is recognized by his nurse

_____ 20. ELPENOR — T. God of the sun; owner of the cattle which Odysseus' men ate

Odyssey Multiple Choice Unit Test 2 Page 2

II. Multiple Choice
1. Why had Odysseus not yet returned home from the Trojan War?
    A. He had angered the god Poseidon by blinding Poseidon's son, Polyphemos. Poseidon has placed obstacles in his way and Odysseus has not yet been able to return home.
    B. His boat had been damaged and he put into a port to have it fixed. The parts he needed were not available so he had to set his men to making them. The process was taking a long time.
    C. He stayed in Troy to help repair the damage done by the war. He felt it was the honorable thing to do.
    D. Odysseus was a man of adventure. He didn't really want to return home to his quiet, dull life, so he set out to have adventures instead.

2. At Odysseus' house in Ithaka, we are introduced to the suitors. What are they doing in the house?
    A. They are looking for eligible partners among Penelope's servant girls.
    B. They are offering their condolences to Penelope on the supposed death of Odysseus.
    C. They are waiting for Penelope to make up her mind which one of them she will marry. While waiting, they are eating and drinking all of the food in the house.
    D. They are looking to buy Penelope's fine furniture and household items should she decide to leave the house and move elsewhere.

3. To whom does Athena refer when she says: "They all would find death was quick, and marriage a painful matter?"
    A. She refers to the young virgins in Ithaka.
    B. She refers to the Trojans.
    C. She refers to the widows left after the war.
    D. She refers to the suitors.

4. What happens at the homecoming of Agamemnon?
    A. He is honored by the people and sees his new son for the first time.
    B. He is murdered by his wife, Klytaimnestra, and her lover, Aigisthos.
    C. His family has kept the homecoming a secret so they can greet him privately. He is pleased.
    D. Athena appears and praises him for his bravery.

5. Why is Menelaus to go to the Elysian Field instead of dying as other mortals do?
    A. He is the husband of Helen, and son-in-law of Zeus, and he will not die.
    B. It was a promise that Athena made long ago to his mother.
    C. He is to serve as an inspiration to other mortals, that a valiant and honest life has its rewards.
    D. His offerings to the gods are so far superior that they awarded him that privilege.

Odyssey Multiple Choice Unit Test 2 Page 3

6. Which god or goddess brings a message from Zeus to Kalypso?
    A. Hermes does.
    B. Leukothea, a sea nymph, finds him.
    C. Nausikaa, daughter of Alkinoos, ruler of Skherta, finds Odysseus.
    D. Amphitrite, the chief maid, does.

7. What happens to Odysseus on the eighteenth day, just as he sights the shores of Skheria?
    A. He is attacked by a great whale who swallows the raft. Odysseus manages to swim to safety.
    B. He sees a mirage of a bucket of cool water, created by one of the gods. He is thirsty and drinks most of it, then gets violently ill.
    C. He gets a severe sunburn and falls into a feverish coma. When he awakens he doesn't know where he is.
    D. Poseidon, returning from a vacation in Ethiopia, sees the raft. In a rage he creates a storm which destroys the raft.

8. What help does Ino give to Odysseus?
    A. She give him her magic veil which allows him to survive the long swim to Skheria.
    B. She sends a pod of dolphins to surround and protect his ship.
    C. She creates a magic ship for him.
    D. She calms the wind so the waves are not too big.

9. Odysseus is insulted by Seareach. What does he accuse Odysseus of being?
    A. Seareach accuses Odysseus of being a spy who wants to steal the secrets of the Phaikians' seafaring skills.
    B. Seareach accuses Odysseus of being a man concerned only with business and profits and not with being an athlete.
    C. He accuses Odysseus of being a fortune-hunter who only wants to marry a rich wife and live comfortably on her wealth.
    D. He accuses Odysseus of being a curse sent from the gods to destroy their way of life.

10. Why is it necessary for Odysseus to take some of his men by force away from the land of the Lotos-Eaters?
    A. The lotos fruit paralyzed them and they were not able to leave by themselves.
    B. The lotos fruit gave them panic attacks. They became fearful of embarking on another sea voyage.
    C. The lotos fruit contained a magical drug that made them want to stay and eat more.
    D. The lotos fruit made them fall in love with the women of the land and not want to leave.

Odyssey Multiple Choice Unit Test 2 Page 4

11. How is Odysseus able to wound Polyphemos?
    A. Odysseus poisons the wine and makes Polyphemos so sick that he is unable to defend himself.
    B. Odysseus drives his sword through Polyphemos' liver.
    C. Odysseus and his men use a log sharpened on one end and drive it into his eye while he sleeps.
    D. Odysseus and his men set Polyphemos on fire while he is milking the goats.

12. Odysseus and his men come within sight of Ithaka. Why do they not land?
    A. They are afraid they will not be remembered and will be killed as intruders.
    B. They want to wait until they have time to clean up and properly prepare themselves.
    C. The ship is sunk on a reef.
    D. The men think the bag from Aeolus contains treasure that Odysseus is keeping for himself. While Odysseus is sleeping, they open the bag. The winds escape and they are blown back to the Aeolan island.

13. Why must Odysseus visit the house of Hades?
    A. He must consult with the blind prophet Teiresias, who will tell Odysseus all he needs to know about getting home.
    B. He has to get magical supplies for his ship, and Hades is the only place to get them.
    C. He must atone for his past misbehavior before he can go home.
    D. He has to deliver the dead crewmen.

14. What does Odysseus promise Elpenor?
    A. He promises to tell of Elpenor's brave deeds wherever he tells the story of his own adventures.
    B. He promises to return to Kirke's island and bury Elpenor's body.
    C. He promises to take care of Elpenor's wife and children.
    D. He promises to avenge Elpenor's death.

15. How do Odysseus and his men avoid destruction by the Seirines?
    A. They throw trinkets and pieces of brightly colored cloth onto the island. The Seirines are fascinated with these items and forget to sing.
    B. They sing their own songs in the loudest possible voices, to drown out the sound of the Seirines.
    C. Athena puts all of the men into a magical sleep and guides the boat through herself.
    D. Odysseus orders his men to plug their ears with beeswax and has them lash him to the mast.

Odyssey Multiple Choice Unit Test 2 Page 5

16. Telemakhos receives an omen as he is about to depart. What is it, and what does it mean?
    A. A mountain eagle holding a white goose in its talons flies to the right over the horses. Helen interprets the sign to mean that Odysseus will soon return to Ithaka and take revenge on the suitors.
    B. He sees a double rainbow over the bow of the ship. He thinks it is a good luck sign, that he will have a safe journey.
    C. Three dark clouds travel across the sun. Those who see it think it means that something terrible will happen in three days.
    D. A pod of dolphins surround the ship. The crew thinks this means that they are at last in Poseidon's good graces.

17. Odysseus has a plan that he shares with Eumaios. What is it?
    A. Odysseus plans to go to his own house and ask for a job as a servant for the suitors.
    B. He will disguise himself as a suitor and try to win Penelope himself.
    C. Odysseus will dress in his finest clothing and boldly enter his house.
    D. He will go to town and talk to the families of the suitors and ask them to remove the suitors from his house.

18. What instructions does Odysseus give to Telemakhos?
    A. He tells him to take Penelope away into a special hiding place in the woods and wait for a signal when it will be safe to come back. He says not to tell anyone else of the hiding place and to make sure they are not followed.
    B. He tells him to go home and wait for his father's arrival as a beggar. He warns Telemakhos not to interfere if the suitors are rude but to wait for the signal to hide all weapons except their own. He also reminds Telemakhos not to let anyone know that he (Odysseus) has returned.
    C. He tells him to go home and act like a madman and threaten the suitors. Then he should lock himself and Penelope in her quarters and send his servant to Odysseus when this has been accomplished.
    D. He tells Telemakhos to go to the house disguised as another suitor. He should try to get the others into jealous quarrels and keep them distracted.

19. What occurs between Odysseus and Iros? Why?
    A. They have a fist fight to decide which beggar may stay and which may leave.
    B. They have a debate on who the most promising suitor is.
    C. Iros thinks he recognizes the beggar as Odysseus. Odysseus has to deny it and distract Iros by talking about food and women.
    D. They plot together to rob Penelope's house and blame it on the suitors.

Odyssey Multiple Choice Unit Test 2 Page 6

20. What does Penelope do that makes Odysseus happy?
    A. She refuses to see the suitors and banishes all of them to the courtyard.
    B. She tells the suitors she will never marry again, even if Odysseus is dead.
    C. She enriches the house by requesting expensive gifts from the suitors.
    D. She offers sacrifice to the gods and prays for her husband's safe return.

21. What contest does Penelope devise to test the suitors?
    A. She says she will marry the man who wins against all of the others in a sword fight to the death.
    B. She says she will marry the man who will give her her weight in gold.
    C. She tells them that whoever is able to move her husband's bed shall be her husband.
    D. She decides whoever can string the great bow of Odysseus and send an arrow through the iron of twelve axes shall be her husband.

22. How does Penelope test Odysseus?
    A. She asks for details of their wedding and the birth of Telemakhos.
    B. She asks him to name all of her relatives.
    C. She tells the servants to bring out his bed, and then waits for his reaction.
    D. She has Eurycleia identify him, and then inspects the scar on his leg herself.

23. What does Athena do when the families of the dead suitors attack Odysseus?
    A. She kills all of the male relatives of the suitors.
    B. She makes Odysseus give gifts to the families of the suitors.
    C. She puts a protective mist around Odysseus so his enemies can't hurt him.
    D. She makes both sides pledge peace.

Odyssey Multiple Choice Unit Test 2 Page 7

III. Composition

1. Explain the structure of the narrative. Use graphic organizers such as a time line or a book map if you need them.

2. Compare and contrast the significance of the adventures that Odysseus had in the nine years prior to his stay with Kalypso with the adventures he had after leaving her island. Which are more important?

3. Identify the qualities that were most important for a man to have in Odysseus' time and give examples from *The Odyssey* of those who exemplified each.

Odyssey Multiple Choice Unit Test 2 Page 8

IV. Vocabulary - Match the correct definitions to the words.

_____ 1. STEEPED   A. Kind

_____ 2. PUNGENT   B. Priority; going in advance

_____ 3. VIE   C. Stubbornness

_____ 4. RANCOR   D. Having a sharp, bitter taste

_____ 5. STALWART   E. Soaked

_____ 6. DOLE   F. To distribute in small portions

_____ 7. GUILE   G. To compete or strive for victory

_____ 8. CALAMITOUS   H. Robbed of goods by force

_____ 9. BENEVOLENT   I. Treacherous cunning; craftiness

_____ 10. PRECEDENCE   J. Brilliant

_____ 11. VIVACITY   K. To assemble or gather

_____ 12. MUSTER   L. Concealing or disguising

_____ 13. OBSTINACY   M. Liveliness

_____ 14. CHATTELS   N. An inheritance from a father

_____ 15. CODDLED   O. Causing or involving disaster

_____ 16. PATRIMONY   P. Bitter, long-lasting resentment

_____ 17. PLUNDERED   Q. Watchfulness

_____ 18. VIGILANCE   R. Treated indulgently; babied

_____ 19. DISSIMULATION   S. Articles of personal, movable property

_____ 20. RESPLENDENT   T. Having physical strength

ANSWER SHEET - *The Odyssey*
Multiple Choice Unit Tests

I. Matching	II. Multiple Choice	IV. Vocabulary
1. ___	1. ___	1. ___
2. ___	2. ___	2. ___
3. ___	3. ___	3. ___
4. ___	4. ___	4. ___
5. ___	5. ___	5. ___
6. ___	6. ___	6. ___
7. ___	7. ___	7. ___
8. ___	8. ___	8. ___
9. ___	9. ___	9. ___
10. ___	10. ___	10. ___
11. ___	11. ___	11. ___
12. ___	12. ___	12. ___
13. ___	13. ___	13. ___
14. ___	14. ___	14. ___
15. ___	15. ___	15. ___
16. ___	16. ___	16. ___
17. ___	17. ___	17. ___
18. ___	18. ___	18. ___
19. ___	19. ___	19. ___
20. ___	20. ___	20. ___
	21. ___	
	22. ___	
	23. ___	

ANSWER KEY - *The Odyssey*
Multiple Choice Unit Tests

I. Matching		II. Multiple Choice		IV. Vocabulary	
1. H	Q	1. B	A	1. N	E
2. K	C	2. D	C	2. R	D
3. P	G	3. C	D	3. J	G
4. C	T	4. C	B	4. A	P
5. N	F	5. D	A	5. Q	T
6. Q	H	6. B	A	6. B	F
7. G	O	7. B	D	7. P	I
8. R	N	8. C	A	8. E	O
9. T	K	9. C	B	9. D	A
10. D	J	10. A	C	10. I	B
11. O	R	11. B	C	11. O	M
12. B	S	12. C	D	12. H	K
13. S	M	13. B	A	13. G	C
14. F	P	14. A	B	14. C	S
15. I	I	15. A	D	15. M	R
16. M	E	16. C	A	16. S	N
17. E	L	17. C	A	17. T	H
18. L	B	18. C	B	18. F	Q
19. A	D	19. B	A	19. L	L
20. J	A	20. D	C	20. K	J
		21. B	D		
		22. B	C		
		23. C	D		

UNIT RESOURCE MATERIALS

BULLETIN BOARD IDEAS - *The Odyssey*

1. Save one corner of the board for the best of students' *The Odyssey* writing assignments.

2. Take one of the word search puzzles from the extra activities packet and with a marker copy it over in a large size on the bulletin board. Write the clue words to find to one side. Invite students prior to and after class to find the words and circle them on the bulletin board.

3. Write several of the most significant quotations from the book onto the board on brightly colored paper.

4. Make a bulletin board listing the vocabulary words for this unit. As you complete sections of the novel and discuss the vocabulary for each section, write the definitions on the bulletin board. (If your board is one students face frequently, it will help them learn the words.)

5. Make a collage. Students find pictures of famous present-day people who resemble (physically or in personality) the characters in *The Odyssey*. They cut out the pictures and paste them on a piece of paper. Under the picture, they write the name of the character being represented. A variation would be to section the bulletin board so that each of the major characters has a space. Put the name of the character at the top of the space. Invite students to post their pictures of famous people in the appropriate space. Thus, you may have three or four different personalities in the Odyssey. (How about Sylvester Stallone or Hulk Hogan for Odysseus!) Encourage discussion so that students can defend their choices (perhaps one student chooses Princess Diana as a representative for Penelope and another chooses her for Athena).

6. Make a time line of Odysseus' journey. Make another timeline of the concurrent events in Ithaka, including the journey of Telemakhos. Align the two timelines to get a clearer picture of how the events coordinated.

7. Display a map of ancient Greece and have students use yarn to show the route of Odysseus' journey.

8. Have the students write "Personals Ads" from the various suitors, telling why they should be chosen by Penelope. Each ad should be numbered. Have a contest and have students vote for their favorite ads.

9. Make a bulletin board about Greek history.

Bulletin Board Ideas Continued *The Odyssey*

10. Make a travel bulletin board for Greece. See your local travel agent for some materials.

11. Make a little "Book" (single page of construction paper folded over) with the name of a character from Greek mythology. Place the name of the character on the front of the book and write a little biography of the character inside. This also makes a good introductory activity for students to do--then all you have to do is post them on the board.

12. Post pictures of Bronze Age weapons, ships, people, dishes, art, etc. on the board.

EXTRA ACTIVITIES - *The Odyssey*

One of the difficulties in teaching a novel is that all students don't read at the same speed. One student who likes to read may take the book home and finish it in a day or two. Sometimes a few students finish the in-class assignments early. The problem, then, is finding suitable extra activities for students.

The best thing I've found is to keep a little library in the classroom. For this unit on *The Odyssey*, you might check out from the school library *The Oresteia* by Aeschylus, *The Iliad* by Homer, "The Quest for Ulysses" in *National Geographic* August 1986, Vol. 170 No. 2, *In Search of the Trojan War* by Michael Wood, *Electra* or *Philoctetes* by Sophocles, *The Shield of Achilles* by W. H. Auden, or some of these works by Euripides: *Helen, Electra, The Trojan Women,* or *Hecabe*. Also, criticism of Homer's works would be appropriate. Any stories of Greek mythology, articles about Greece, ship building, famous Greeks, religion in Greece through the centuries, mystical creatures of the sea (such as mermaids, etc.), Greek ceremonies, Greek cooking, travel information about Greece, Greek architecture, athletics, musical instruments, or articles about the archeological studies done in the area would also be of interest.

Other things you may keep on hand are puzzles. We have made some relating directly to *The Odyssey* for you. Feel free to duplicate them.

Some students may like to draw. You might devise a contest or allow some extra-credit grade for students who draw characters or scenes from *The Odyssey*. Note, too, that if the students do not want to keep their drawings you may pick up some extra bulletin board materials this way. If you have a contest and you supply the prize (a CD or something like that perhaps), you could, possibly, make the drawing itself a non-returnable entry fee.

The pages which follow contain games, puzzles and worksheets. The keys, when appropriate, immediately follow the puzzle or worksheet. There are two main groups of activities: one group for the unit; that is, generally relating to *The Odyssey* text and another group of activities related strictly to *The Odyssey* vocabulary.

Directions for these games, puzzles and worksheets are self-explanatory. The object here is to provide you with extra materials you may use in any way you choose.

MORE ACTIVITIES - *The Odyssey*

1. Have students work together to make a time line chronology of the events in the story. Take a large piece of construction paper and on one wall (or however you can physically arrange it in your room) make the events of the story along it. Students may want to add drawings or cut-out pictures to represent the events (as well as a written statement).

2. Have students design a book cover (front and back and inside flaps) for *The Odyssey*.

3. Have students design a bulletin board (ready to be put up; not just sketched) for *The Odyssey*.

4. Have students group the books together to show the larger structure of the novel. Have them explain why they chose the divisions they made.

5. Have students choose one book of the epic (with sufficient dialogue) to rewrite as a play. In conjunction with this assignment, have students write a composition explaining the difficulties they encountered in changing from one written form to another.

6. Have a Greece Day during which you explore the history, culture and other aspects of Greece.

7. Have students compare the main characters in *The Odyssey* with those of another epic-type novel or a television series.

8. Write a song or a rap about (one of) Odysseus' adventures.

9. Design a series of postcards that Odysseus could have sent home from his journeys. On one side, draw a picture of the land where he has stopped. On the other side, have him write a note to his family about the adventure.

10. Find another translation or translations of *The Odyssey*. Compare the different spellings of the names of many of the main characters and places. Make a list of these and discuss possible reasons for so many different spellings.

11. Have a costume day. Invite students to dress up as one of the characters in the book. The students must then keep the persona of that character. Students can talk to each other about the events in the epic, but only in character.

More Activities *The Odyssey* Continued

12. Play an identity game. Write the names of the characters on index cards, one per card. Tape one card on each student's back. Each student will have to guess his or her identity by talking to other students, gathering information about his or her character. (Students may not ask, "Who am I?") Those who correctly identify their characters can then put their name tags on the front. Play can continue until all students have identified their characters, or a specified amount of time could be set.

13. Have students memorize the Greek alphabet.

14. Have students use maps of the ancient world and trace Odysseus' route. Then have them compare the route on modern maps.

WORD SEARCH - *The Odyssey*

All words in this list are associated with *The Odyssey*. The words are placed backwards, forward, diagonally, up and down. The included words are listed below the word searches.

```
G C N B P A H Y S B Y S F A D K A H F F O S K T
D V R H W Q E M R C L A E R N N M R V W U M Q T
W D U O R H S O H K A M E L E T O L A E R T E S
V M N X S K T O L K L R E H G T I L Z D K U P N
F I T Z H S E S I U X Y T N N A L N K H R R R R
L Y Z E E U B S N L S A T E E Y E S O Y E R I D
A P R N M A U O T A E S M A K L L D M O D L N K
S I C A K A D F W F I H U S M O A A I L S O E K
A P E A N Y X D L D I N F G T N C U R S D P Q N
H U H L S M S D B B P G O O R H E O S I C S F B
S T X S K E M Y H E X O S G O A W S E E U R S
I H E B T Y R P N M S E L S Y R G S T N D K S M
G U Y S B A R E J A A E S Y E R O A I R S A W D
S J E D H O L U I T W N P D P P T R M O A O H S
F R L K N O B S E J A L N O S H I S O E S J R R
O M P E P P E R N I V U F M L E E N E P M O X H
Y V P E M R S F A T H H G T S K I M Y A T N H W
G L F Q I L G H T Z D G L Q V K Y L O I L W O Y
E R F E H Y K P T L F M Q G L J A K U S G B B N
K D T B B A G X T W Z Q S A G K H S Y F K C V W
```

AGAMEMNON	EURYKLEIA	KYKLOPES	POLYPHEMOS
AEOLUS	EURYMACHOS	LAERTES	POSEIDON
AKHAIANS	GIFTS	LAESTRYGONIANS	SCAR
ALKINOOS	HADES	LOTOSEATERS	SEIRINES
ANTINOOS	HELEN	MENELAUS	SHROUD
ARGUS	HELIOS	MENTOR	SKHERIA
ATHENA	INO	NAUSIKAA	SKYLLA
CROSSBOW	ITHAKA	NESTOR	SUITORS
DISCUS	KALYPSO	ODYSSEUS	TEIRESIAS
EAGLE	KHARYBDIS	OMEN	TELEMAKHOS
ELPENOR	KIRKE	ORESTES	UNDERWORLD
EUMAEUS		PENELOPE	ZEUS

CROSSWORD *The Odyssey*

CROSSWORD CLUES *The Odyssey*

ACROSS
1. Goddess who kept Odysseus on her island for years
5. Helen's husband; King of Sparta
8. Plate-like object that is thrown in contests
10. King of the gods; lives on Mt. Olympus
12. Goddess who gave Odysseus her veil
14. The one-eyed giants
19. Sign of good or bad luck to come
20. Home of the Phaikians
22. Odysseus's dog
24. Ruler of the underworld; brother to Zeus and Poseidon
26. Bird often used as omen
28. One of Homer's names for the Greeks
32. Daughter of the King of Phaikia
33. One of Odysseus's crew; fell from Kirke's roof
34. Wife of Menelaus; the Prince of Troy abducted her
35. The men who wanted to marry Penelope

DOWN
2. God of the sea; seeks revenge on Odysseus for blinding his son
3. Hero of the Trojan War who goes on a journey
4. Nurse for both Odysseus & Telemakhos
5. A visitor in Ithaka; rally Athena disguised
6. A mortal to whom the gods have given control of the winds
7. Nymphs whose singing entices men to land on their island
9. Means by which Odysseus is recognized by nurse
11. One of the suitors; threw a stool at Odysseus
13. God of the sun; owner of cattle
15. Whirlpool that sucked down ship and crewmen
16. Blind prophet whom Odysseus visited in the underworld
17. Father of Odysseus
18. Agamemnon's son
20. Six-headed monster
21. Native land and home of Odysseus
23. Guarded by Hades; the place where the dead go
25. Faithful wife of Odysseus
27. Odysseus's faithful swineherd
29. Goddess who tried to turn Odysseus & crew into pigs
30. King of Pylos; reminisces about the good old days
31. They were important to the Greeks; presents

CROSSWORD ANSWER KEY *The Odyssey*

MATCHING QUIZ/WORKSHEET 1 - *The Odyssey*

____ 1. KHARYBDIS A. Race of cannibals

____ 2. EURYMACHOS B. A whirlpool that sucked down ship & crewmen

____ 3. MENTOR C. Goddess who kept Odysseus on her island for many years

____ 4. MENELAUS D. The Kyklops who captured Odysseus and his men & was blinded by them

____ 5. LAESTRYGONIANS E. God of the sea; seeks revenge on Odysseus for blinding his son

____ 6. EURYKLEIA F. Goddess who gave Odysseus her veil to keep him afloat

____ 7. ALKINOOS G. A hero of the Trojan War & main character in The Odyssey

____ 8. AKHAIANS H. King of the Phaiakians; gives Odysseus passage to Ithaka

____ 9. ORESTES I. King of Pylos; reminisces frequently about the good old days

____ 10. HELEN J. The men who wanted to marry Penelope

____ 11. POSEIDON K. Wife of Menelaus; the prince of Troy abducted her

____ 12. INO L. Sign of good or bad luck to come

____ 13. NESTOR M. Odysseus' faithful swineherd; helped Odysseus kill the suitors

____ 14. ODYSSEUS N. One of the suitors; insults Odysseus & throws a stool at him

____ 15. KALYPSO O. A visitor in Ithaka; really Athena disguised in his form

____ 16. SUITORS P. One of Homer's names for the Greeks

____ 17. POLYPHEMOS Q. Nurse for both Odysseus and Telemakhos

____ 18. OMEN R. Agamemnon's son who took revenge for his father's death

____ 19. EUMAEUS S. Father of Odysseus

____ 20. LAERTES T. Helen's husband; King of Sparta

MATCHING QUIZ/WORKSHEET 2 - *The Odyssey*

____ 1. INO   A. Agamemnon's son who took revenge for his father's death

____ 2. ODYSSEUS   B. One of Odysseus' crew; was drunk & fell from Kirke's roof

____ 3. DISCUS   C. A mortal to whom the gods have given control of the winds

____ 4. HADES   D. A hero of the Trojan War & main character in The Odyssey

____ 5. EURYMACHOS   E. Wife of Menelaus; the prince of Troy abducted her

____ 6. ORESTES   F. A visitor in Ithaka; really Athena disguised in his form

____ 7. POLYPHEMOS   G. One of the suitors; insults Odysseus & throws a stool at him

____ 8. SKHERIA   H. One of Homer's names for the Greeks

____ 9. HELIOS   I. The Kyklops who captured Odysseus and his men & was wounded by them

____ 10. AEOLUS   J. King of Pylos; reminisces frequently about the good old days

____ 11. ELPENOR   K. God of the sun; owner of the cattle which Odysseus' men ate

____ 12. UNDERWORLD   L. A plate-like object that is thrown in contests

____ 13. LAERTES   M. King of Mycene; leader of Greeks during Trojan War; murdered by his wife & her lover

____ 14. SKYLLA   N. Home of the Phaikians

____ 15. KYKLOPES   O. Ruler of the underworld; brother to Zeus and Poseidon

____ 16. HELEN   P. The one-eyed giants

____ 17. AKHAIANS   Q. Goddess who gave Odysseus her veil to keep him afloat

____ 18. AGAMEMNON   R. Father of Odysseus

____ 19. MENTOR   S. Guarded by Hades; the place where the dead go

____ 20. NESTOR   T. Six headed monster who sits across from the Kharybdis

KEY: MATCHING QUIZ/WORKSHEETS - *The Odyssey*

Worksheet 1	Worksheet 2
1. B	1. Q
2. N	2. D
3. O	3. L
4. T	4. O
5. A	5. G
6. Q	6. A
7. H	7. I
8. P	8. N
9. R	9. K
10. K	10. C
11. E	11. B
12. F	12. S
13. I	13. R
14. G	14. T
15. C	15. P
16. J	16. E
17. D	17. H
18. L	18. M
19. M	19. F
20. S	20. J

JUGGLE LETTER REVIEW GAME CLUE SHEET - *The Odyssey*

SCRAMBLED	WORD	CLUE
RESTEOS	ORESTES	Agamemnon's son
KELYSOPK	KYKLOPES	The one-eyed giants
KLASLY	SKYLLA	Six headed monster
IAKNASUA	NAUSIKAA	Daughter of the king of Phaikia
RETASLE	LAERTES	Father of Odysseus
UEEUASM	EUMAEUS	Odysseus' faithful swineheard
NSELAUME	MENELAUS	Helen's husband; King of Sparta
LNORPEE	ELPENOR	One of Odysseus' crew; fell from Kirke's roof
SORCWOSB	CROSSBOW	Weapon of Odysseus
LHENE	HELEN	Wife of Menelaus; the Prince of Troy abducted her
SOIEHL	HELIOS	God of the sun; owner of cattle
AYSANTEKLMTRI	KLYTIAMNESTRA	Wife and murderer of Agamemnon
ESZU	ZEUS	King of the gods; lives on Mt. Olympus
LEAEG	EAGLE	Bird often used as an omen
AAKHTI	ITHAKA	Native land and home of Odysseus
DYSESSOU	ODYSSEUS	Hero of the Trojan War; main character of *Odyssey*
CARS	SCAR	Means by which Odysseus is recognized by nurse
TFSIG	GIFTS	They were important to the Greeks; presents
EOUSLA	AEOLUS	A mortal to whom the gods have given control of the winds
ERKIK	KIRKE	Goddess who tried to turn Odysseus & crew into pigs
ERNISIES	SEIRINES	Nymphs whose singing entices men to land on their island
SKOPLAY	KALYPSO	Goddess who kept Odysseus on her island for years
GURSA	ARGUS	Odysseus' dog
USISCD	DISCUS	A plate-like object that is thrown in contests
DYIAHRKSB	KHARYBDIS	A whirlpool that sucked down ship and crewmen
ORRDLEUDNW	UNDERWORLD	Guarded by Hades; the place where the dead go
ASYOREHCUM	EURYMACHOS	One of the suitors; throws a stool at Odysseus
IHAKNSAA	AKHAIANS	One of Homer's names for the Greeks
NOME	OMEN	Sign of good or bad luck to come
MNMNAOEGA	AGAMEMNON	King of Mycene; murdered by his wife & her lover
ERTEASSII	TEIRESIAS	Blind prophet whom Odysseus visited in the underworld
ELENPEOP	PENELOPE	Faithful wife of Odysseus
RTENSO	NESTOR	King of Pylos; reminisces about the good old days
EORMNT	MENTOR	A visitor in Ithaka; really Athena disguised
NOI	INO	Goddess who gave Odysseus her veil

VOCABULARY RESOURCE MATERIALS

VOCABULARY WORD SEARCH - *The Odyssey*

All words in this list are associated with *The Odyssey* with an emphasis on the vocabulary words chosen for study in the text. The words are placed backwards, forward, diagonally, up and down. The included words are listed below.

```
D H V F Q T F K V C S Y C O E D M R W D V X E
A P P A L L E D I M P L A C A B L E C O M E L Y
P G R O U I U G E U O C A U A L L I R F D O I Q
F A U O G S I M N L H R D R G N A I U E D N Z V
S T T N M L P G I E D A T P I U I M V G L N A W
Q U B R A O E I K N C D V I R O R T I I W I J C
I B C N I N N U C I O N O A F O N Y S T O S C H
D N C C T M B T T I T U E C L I F R B O N F T
M E S P U E O Y O P O I S R M O E U H A O U Y L
S E P I R M C N R R E U M U E N R D S I N T S X
P T A E D V B N Y E Y R S O E F V V T I I C W X
Z I A G E I F E E P S T P V R S E A H C O H O D
W J T L E T O K D D E P O L M O L D A H S N E R
L I S H W R S U F R E L L F E U U V C L M R J C
Z N N B K A H V S F E C C E M X I S E Y E S B M
N G D D N M R K R N R H E I N V I T X D H V L F
R Z L F F D P T T S F S S R C D T T N P Q B Q T
P V M N X A H G C D M S T X P A E U Y R C B Z L
M J S B V Q L S F G I G Z M H W L N T M Z H F Z
S P J G Q Z X L V D L T J C S P G S T D J S J M
```

APPALLED	DEFERENCE	MUSTER	REBUKE
AUDACITY	DERELICT	OBLIVION	RESPLENDENT
AUGURY	DISSIMULATION	OBSTINACY	STALWART
AUSPICIOUS	DOLE	PATRIMONY	STEEPED
BENEVOLENT	FEIGN	PERPLEXITY	SUCCUMBED
CACHE	FLOUT	PITH	TIMOROUS
CALAMITOUS	GUILE	PLUNDERED	VALOR
CANDOR	IMPLACABLE	PRECEDENCE	VIE
CHATTELS	INSIDIOUS	PROFUSION	VIGILANCE
CLARION	LUMINOUS	PROMONTORY	VIVACITY
CODDLED	MEAGER	PUNGENT	WINDFALL
COMELY	MORTIFIED	RANCOR	

VOCABULARY CROSSWORD *The Odyssey*

VOCABULARY CROSSWORD CLUES *The Odyssey*

ACROSS
3 Filled with dismay
5 Lizard-like
6 A pair
7 Kind
10 Impressively great in size
12 Vagrant or social outcast
15 Pulled or drawn tight
20 Craftiness
21 Formal conversation
22 Shrill and clear
23 Distribute in small portions
25 Stick on a spinning wheel that holds unspun wool
29 Superior skill or ability
32 Stand on which a coffin or corpse is placed
34 Division, separation
35 Small in quantity, fullness or extent

DOWN
1 Emitting self-generated light
2 Essential or central part of anything
3 The act of destroying completely
4 Axe-like tool with arched blade at right angles to the handle
5 Soaked
6 Water that collects in the low part of a ship's hull
7 Cruel or harsh
8 To compete or strive for victory
9 A person skilled in maneuvering
11 Design incised beneath the surface of metal
12 Scattered in different directions
13 Bitter, long-lasting resentment
14 Hit, toss, or propel in a high arc
16 Brilliant
17 Yielded or submitted to an overpowering force
18 Group of twenty items
19 Beginner or inexperienced person
23 Deserted; dreary; gloomy
24 Boast or brag
26 Restricted or limited
27 Pretend
28 Proper or sound condition; good spirits
30 Criticize sharply
31 Approached an end
33 Empty show; mockery

VOCABULARY CROSSWORD ANSWER KEY *The Odyssey*

Across: APPALLED, BRACE, SAUTIAN (SAUTIAN), BENEVOLENT, PRODIGIOUS, DERELICT, TAUT, GUILE, COLLOQUY, CLARION, DOLE, DISTAFF, PROWESS, BIER, CLEFT, MEAGER

Down: LAMENTED, PANTHEON, DAZZLING, BIG, BRACE, STEEPED, MITIGATE, PITH, HITHER, DISCONSOLATE, RAZE, DIGNITARY, BENIGN, ALLOTMENT, DERELICT, INSPIRE, CONCORD, RECOGNIZABLE, CRESPLENDENT, SUCCUMB, FEET, PROWESS, DOLED, FINANT, STUNTED, GUILE, CLEFT

VOCABULARY WORKSHEET 1 - *The Odyssey*

____ 1. Causing or involving disaster
    A. Perplexity   B. Calamitous   C. Pith   D. Valor

____ 2. Criticize or reprove sharply
    A. Succumbed   B. Auspicious   C. Rebuke   D. Pungent

____ 3. Watchfulness
    A. Vigilance   B. Promontory   C. Augury   D. Mortified

____ 4. Having physical strength
    A. Plundered   B. Audacity   C. Stalwart   D. Coddled

____ 5. Filled with dismay
    A. Obstinacy   B. Deference   C. Appalled   D. Rancor

____ 6. Brilliant
    A. Flout   B. Steeped   C. Resplendent   D. Promontory

____ 7. Interpreting signs and omens
    A. Vie   B. Augury   C. Windfall   D. Succumbed

____ 8. Incapable of appeasement
    A. Rebuke   B. Obstinacy   C. Implacable   D. Auspicious

____ 9. Yielded or submitted to an overpowering force
    A. Coddled   B. Vivacity   C. Luminous   D. Succumbed

____ 10. Attended by favorable circumstances
    A. Chattels   B. Luminous   C. Auspicious   D. Clarion

____ 11. To assemble or gather
    A. Obstinacy   B. Rancor   C. Steeped   D. Muster

____ 12. The state of being puzzled or confused
    A. Perplexity   B. Supplication   C. Promontory   D. Appalled

____ 13. Kind
    A. Benevolent   B. Appalled   C. Candor   D. Chattels

____ 14. A sudden and unexpected piece of good fortune
    A. Resplendent   B. Windfall   C. Meager   D. Valor

____ 15. Stubbornness
    A. Clarion   B. Obstinacy   C. Audacity   D. Promontory

____ 16. A humble or earnest plea
    A. Supplication   B. Resplendent   C. Cache   D. Vigilance

____ 17. Courteous respect
    A. Timorous   B. Chattels   C. Deference   D. Rebuke

____ 18. An inheritance from a father
    A. Plundered   B. Steeped   C. Patrimony   D. Dole

____ 19. A vagrant or social outcast
    A. Dissimulation   B. Auspicious   C. Candor   D. Derelict

____ 20. Articles of personal, movable property
    A. Deference   B. Vigilance   C. Chattels   D. Vivacity

VOCABULARY WORKSHEET 2 - *The Odyssey*

____ 1. PUNGENT   A. Stubbornness

____ 2. PRECEDENCE   B. Courteous respect

____ 3. BENEVOLENT   C. An inheritance from a father

____ 4. CALAMITOUS   D. Having a sharp, bitter taste

____ 5. RESPLENDENT   E. Robbed of goods by force

____ 6. PERPLEXITY   F. To distribute in small portions

____ 7. PROFUSION   G. The state of being puzzled or confused

____ 8. DEFERENCE   H. To assemble or gather

____ 9. PLUNDERED   I. The state of being completely forgotten

____ 10. REBUKE   J. To show contempt or scorn

____ 11. DOLE   K. To compete or strive for victory

____ 12. OBLIVION   L. Kind

____ 13. MUSTER   M. Soaked

____ 14. CONTENTIOUSLY   N. Brilliant

____ 15. FLOUT   O. Causing or involving disaster

____ 16. OBSTINACY   P. Abundance; extravagance

____ 17. PATRIMONY   Q. In a quarrelsome way

____ 18. SUCCUMBED   R. Priority; going in advance

____ 19. VIE   S. Criticize or reprove sharply

____ 20. STEEPED   T. Yielded or submitted to an overpowering force

KEY: VOCABULARY WORKSHEETS - *The Odyssey*

Worksheet 1	Worksheet 2
1. B	1. D
2. C	2. R
3. A	3. L
4. C	4. O
5. C	5. N
6. C	6. G
7. B	7. P
8. C	8. B
9. D	9. E
10. C	10. S
11. D	11. F
12. A	12. I
13. A	13. H
14. B	14. Q
15. B	15. J
16. A	16. A
17. C	17. C
18. C	18. T
19. D	19. K
20. C	20. M

VOCABULARY JUGGLE LETTER REVIEW GAME CLUES - *The Odyssey*

SCRAMBLED	WORD	CLUE
UNPTGEN	PUNGENT	Having a sharp, bitter taste
NORRYOMPOT	PROMONTORY	A high ridge of land jutting into the sea
YTIVAVCI	VIVACITY	Liveliness
EEDRNFCEE	DEFERENCE	Courteous respect
ENDRPCEECE	PRECEDENCE	Priority; going in advance
DEAPAPLL	APPALLED	Filled with dismay
OYCMEL	COMELY	Attractive; handsome; graceful
IMUULNSO	LUMINOUS	Emitting self-generated light
XRLEEPTYPI	PERPLEXITY	The state of being puzzled or confused
PPIAOIUNLCST	SUPPLICATION	A humble or earnest plea
LCTTEASH	CHATTELS	Articles of personal, movable property
LORAV	VALOR	Courage; boldness
UYRGAU	AUGURY	Interpreting signs and omens
UATIDAYC	AUDACITY	Boldness or daring
RUEDNEPDL	PLUNDERED	Robbed of goods by force
OLCDEDD	CODDLED	Treated indulgently; babied
ICUOSPAISU	AUSPICIOUS	Attended by favorable circumstances
OPRMTAYIN	PATRIMONY	An inheritance from a father
RAWATLST	STALWART	Having physical strength
EVI	VIE	To compete or strive for victory
ARCORN	RANCOR	Bitter, long-lasting resentment
LAAPBIMCEL	IMPLACABLE	Incapable of appeasement
IADLLNWF	WINDFALL	A sudden and unexpected piece of good fortune
LTENEBENOV	BENEVOLENT	Kind
IELGU	GUILE	Treacherous cunning; craftiness
RNCIALO	CLARION	Shrill and clear
IORSMUTO	TIMOROUS	Full of apprehensiveness
NOOISPUFR	PROFUSION	Abundance; extravagance
DSPEETE	STEEPED	Soaked
TRMUSE	MUSTER	To assemble or gather
OCDNRA	CANDOR	Frankness; sincerity
DNRNEESTELP	RESPLENDENT	Brilliant
AGELNVCII	VILIGANCE	Watchfulness
KEUBER	REBUKE	Criticize or reprove sharply
MOANSTIILIDSU	DISSIMULATION	Concealing or disguising
NTYSCIOAB	OBSTINACY	Stubbornness
UOTFL	FLOUT	To show contempt or scorn
LEDO	DOLE	To distribute in small portions
GFNIE	FEIGN	To pretend

www.ingramcontent.com/pod-product-compliance
Lightning Source LLC
Chambersburg PA
CBHW051407070526
44584CB00023B/3321